CONTEMPORARY COPPER JEWELRY

STEP-BY-STEP TECHNIQUES AND PROJECTS

SHARILYN MILLER

EDITOR Rebecca Campbell
ART DIRECTOR/DESIGNER Karla Baker
PHOTO DIRECTOR Pamela Norman
PHOTO STYLIST Ann Swanson
TECHNICAL EDITOR Bonnie Brooks
PRODUCTION Katherine Jackson
PHOTOGRAPHY Joe Coca

 Interweave Press LLC
201 East Fourth Street
Loveland, CO 80537-5655
interweavestore.com

Printed in China by Asia Pacific Offset.

Library of Congress Cataloging-in-Publication Data

Miller, Sharilyn.
  Contemporary copper jewelry : step-by-step tech-
niques and projects / Sharilyn Miller.
     p. cm.
  Includes bibliographical references and index.
  ISBN 978-1-59668-143-9 (pbk.)
  1. Jewelry making. 2. Wire craft. 3. Copper jewelry.
I. Title.
  TT212.M5286 2009
  739.27--dc22

                              2009008795

10 9 8 7 6 5 4 3 2 1

CONTEMPORARY COPPER JEWELRY

STEP-BY-STEP TECHNIQUES AND PROJECTS

SHARILYN MILLER

CONTENTS

ACKNOWLEDGMENTS

A book like this is always a communal effort, drawing upon the skills and talents of many individuals besides the author.

First I'd like to thank my editors, Tricia Waddell and Rebecca Campbell, for giving me the opportunity to share new wire-jewelry designs with a larger audience through this book. I'm very thankful for their professional guidance and editorial expertise.

I also appreciate the skills of photographer Joe Coca, who took the step-by-step shots that so helpfully illustrate my written instructions as well as the lovely beauty shots. I'd also like to thank graphic designer Karla Baker and editors Anne Merrow and Bonnie Brooks for their assistance.

Finally, and perhaps most importantly, I must thank contributing artists Dale "Cougar" Armstrong, Eugenia Chan, Rachel Nelson-Smith, and Richard Salley for sharing their unique approach to wire-art jewelry by providing some breathtaking jewelry projects. Thank you, everyone, for helping me to make this new book a reality. I could not have done it without you!

BASIC TECHNIQUES

The following are a few basic techniques you'll find throughout the projects in this book. Throughout the project instructions, you will be referred back to this Basics section. So you can start at the beginning of the book and work your way through the projects—or you can simply pick any project you like best and begin!

WORK-HARDEN YOUR WORK

A good way to work-harden your wire and straighten out any kinks is to hammer it firmly on the bench block with a hard-plastic or rawhide mallet.

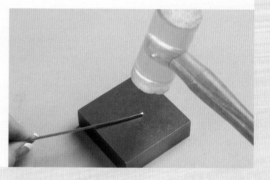

CLEAN YOUR WORK

Before making jewelry, always clean your wire first with a wad of 0000 (superfine) steel wool, which can be found in your local hardware store. Pull of a piece of steel wool from the pad and wad it up, then roll it around on the palm of your hand to compress the fibers. Wrap the ball of steel wool around a length of wire and draw it through, squeezing firmly. This not only cleans your wire, but polishes and straightens it as well.

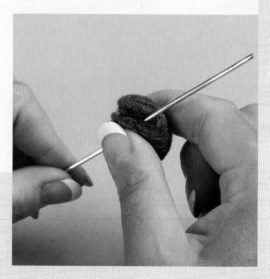

WRAPPED EYE-PIN LOOP

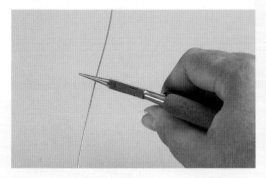

1 To begin a wrapped eye-pin loop, grasp the wire in the round-nose pliers about one-third of the way down from one end of the wire.

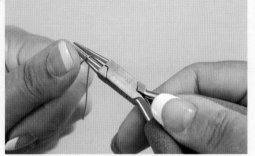

2 Press your nondominant thumb against the wire and turn your hand holding the tool until your wrist is upright.

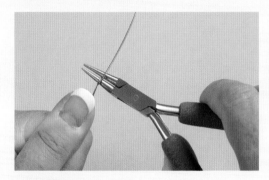

3 Open the tool and bring it around to the original position and then roll the wire around the tool again until you have one complete rotation.

4 Change to chain-nose pliers and grasp the loop in the tips of the tool.

5 Bend the wire back against the edge of the tool.

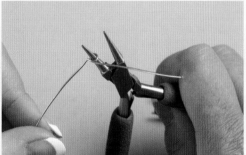

6 Remove the chain-nose pliers and insert the round-nose pliers into the loop.

7 Point the tool straight up and place it in your nondominant hand.

8 Without moving the wire, rotate the tool in your hand until the wire is oriented like a backward L.

9 Grasp the short wire pointing to the left in the tips of the chain-nose pliers.

10 Wrap the short wire up and over the longer wire, turning your hand as you do so to make it easier to wrap.

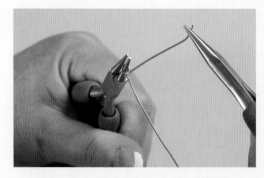

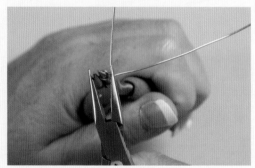

11 Wrap the "neck" area tightly, just beneath the round loop.

12 If necessary, use the tips of the chain-nose pliers to press the first wrap tightly against the loop.

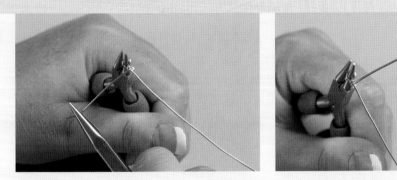

13 Continue wrapping the neck.

14 Wrap the neck up to three times.

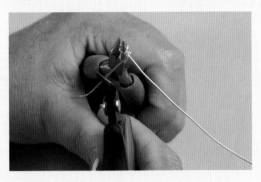

15 If the wire end is too long, it can be trimmed off or it can be spiraled in.

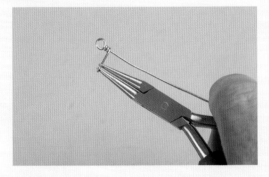

16 To spiral it, start with the tips of the round-nose pliers.

17 Switch to flat-nose pliers and tighten the spiral.

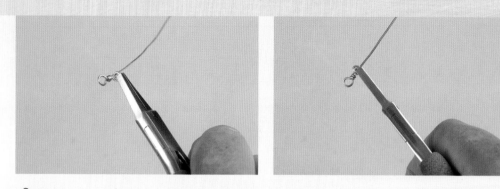

18 Continue spiraling in until you reach the wrapped "neck" area.

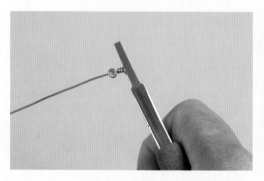

19 Place the round single-wrapped eye-pin loop in the flat-nose pliers and press firmly to improve its shape.

20 Hammering the loop is optional.

FLUSH CUT

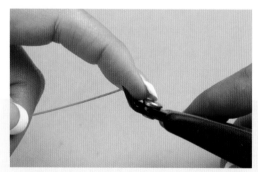

1 To flush cut wire, always place a finger or thumb over the tip of the wire to keep it from shooting away and hitting you or someone else. Notice that the flat side of the blade is oriented toward the long length of wire.

2 Once one end of the wire is flush cut, use a ruler or measuring tape to flush cut the opposite end at a precise measurement of your choosing. Notice that the flat side of the blade is facing the short end of the wire.

FRENCH WRAPPED EAR HOOK

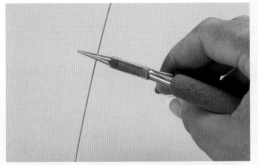

1 Making a French wrapped ear hook is very similar to starting a single-wrapped eye-pin loop. Flush cut about 4" (10 cm) of 22-gauge or 20-gauge wire and place the wire in the round-nose pliers at the one-third and two-thirds positions.

2 Place your thumb against the wire and roll your wrist around, bending a loop in the wire. Notice that the short end of the wire comes to the right of the long end.

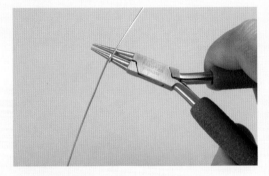

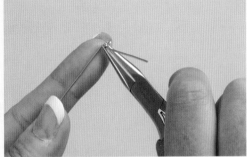

3 Continue bending the wire around until you have a complete loop.

4 Break the "neck" area beneath the loop by pressing your index finger against the wire.

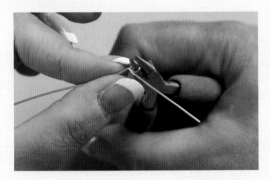

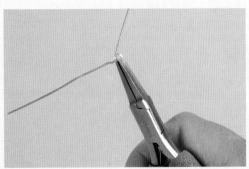

5 Reinsert the round-nose pliers all the way into the loop so that you can adjust it, ensuring that the straight wire is positioned directly beneath the loop.

6 Use flat-nose pliers to open the loop sideways.

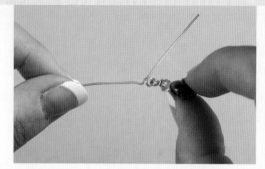

7 Place a bead dangle on the opened loop.

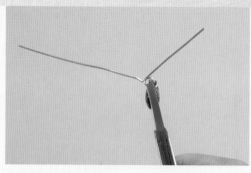

8 Use flat-nose pliers to close the loop sideways.

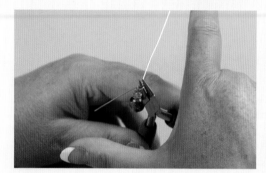

9 Point the tool straight up and place it in your nondominant hand. Without moving the wire, rotate the tool in your hand until the wire is oriented like a backward L.

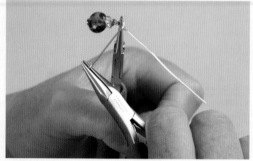

10 Begin wrapping the neck tightly against the loop.

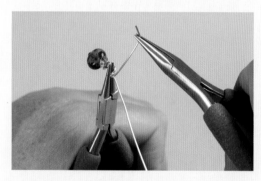

11 Continue wrapping.

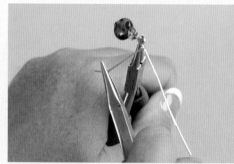

12 Wrap around another time.

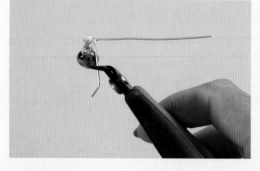

13 Flush cut any excess wire if necessary.

14 Begin spiraling in the wire end.

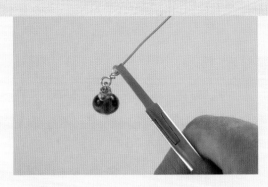

15 Finish the spiral in the tips of the flat-nose pliers.

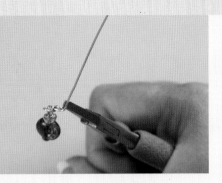

16 Bend the wire over the spiral.

17 Turn the wire over so that it is pointing toward you and place it in either large round-nose or bail-forming pliers.

18 Here is another view of the correct orientation.

19 Bend the wire up and over the tool, pressing tightly against it, to form a perfect ear hook.

20 Bend the last ¼" (.64 cm) back slightly to make the ear hook easier to put through an earlobe.

OPTION: Forge the rounded area of the ear hook very carefully with a chasing hammer; don't hammer it down too thin or it will be like a razor blade in your ear! Another option is to work-harden (see page 8) the ear hook by hammering it with a hard-plastic mallet instead of a chasing hammer.

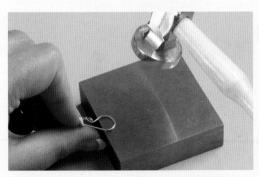

SPIRAL-TRIANGLE CHARM

1 To make a spiral-triangle charm, start by spiraling in a 6" (15 cm) piece of 20-gauge wire. Then grasp the spiral in flat-nose pliers as shown and bend a sharp angle into the wire.

2 Press the edge of the flat-nose pliers against the spiral and bend another angle.

3 Repeat once more to create a triangle with a spiral inside.

4 Bend the wire straight up out of the spiral.

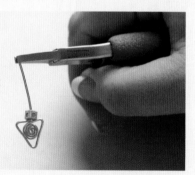

5 Place a bead on the wire.

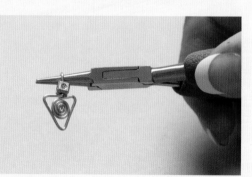

OPTION: Use round-nose pliers to bend the wire over in a small loop so that it can be attached to a jewelry piece.

SMOOTHING WIRE

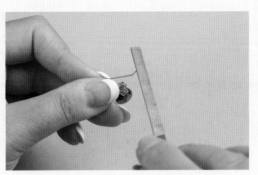

1 To smooth the cut end of the wire, use a cup burr in your handheld drill or flex shaft.

2 Lacking a cup burr, you can use a jeweler's flat file to smooth the wire end instead.

AGING METAL

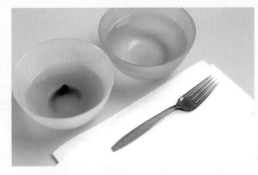

1 To artificially age sterling silver, copper, or brass jewelry, gather your materials: two glass bowls, a chip or two of liver of sulfur, a plastic fork, and some paper towels.

2 Pour very hot (but not boiling) water into the bowl with liver of sulfur. Pour tepid water into the other bowl. Wait until the sulfur chip dissolves.

3 You can stir the sulfur solution with a fork to hasten this action.

4 Run plain hot water over your jewelry to heat the metal and then dip it into the sulfur solution. Using a fork is helpful and protects your fingers from the liver of sulfur.

5 In just a few moments the metal (copper or silver) will darken to a gunmetal gray color. Yellow brass will also darken in this solution, but only slightly, to a brownish yellow color.

6 Dip the jewelry piece in tepid water to rinse.

7 Once rinsed, place the jewelry piece on a paper towel to dry.

8 The piece may be allowed to air-dry or can be hand-dried with a towel.

9 Wad up a piece of 0000 steel wool and rub it briskly all over the jewelry piece.

POLISHING

1 Polishing with steel wool removes the blackening from the surface areas of the wire, leaving it dark in all the little nooks and crannies. This brings out the character in your jewelry.

2 Polish carefully all over the jewelry piece, front and back.

3 A small brass brush can be used to remove any bits of steel wool from the polished jewelry.

4 Use a jeweler's polishing cloth to clean your polished jewelry and make it shine.

copper spiral
Bracelet with wire charms

SHARILYN MILLER

Thick clusters of handmade wire charms and bead dangles make this bracelet as fun to make as it is to wear.

FINISHED SIZE: *8" (20.3 cm)*

MATERIALS

Toggle clasp

64 copper head pins

5' (152 cm) of round dead-soft copper 18-gauge wire

6' (183 cm) of round dead-soft copper 20-gauge wire

8 dark amethyst 7x10mm diamond-shaped beads

8 silver 4mm rounds

8 hematite 4mm rondelles

8 labradorite 6x9mm faceted rectangles

8 labradorite 8mm faceted rectangles

8 Thai silver 4mm cornerless cubes

8 Thai silver 4mm cubes

8 black 6mm faceted rondelles

TOOLS

Toggle clasp

Flush cutters

Measuring tape

0000 steel wool

Chasing hammer

Small bench block

Small round-nose pliers

Flat-nose pliers

Chain-nose pliers

STEP 1: Clean all the wire thoroughly with 0000 steel wool (see Basics section pp. 8–19). To make a triangle-spiral charm, start by flush cutting (see Basics section pp. 8–19) 6" (15.2 cm) of 20-gauge wire. Spiral it in three times, and then grasp it in the flat-nose pliers as shown to bend the wire straight against the spiral.

STEP 2: Grasp the wire and bend it again, firmly against the spiral.

STEP 3: Repeat one more time.

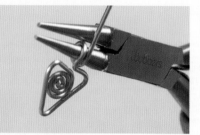

STEP 4: Bend the wire straight up from the triangle-spiral.

STEP 5: Bend a loop in the wire above the triangle-spiral, near the back of the small round-nose pliers.

STEP 6: Break the neck.

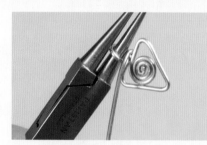

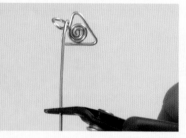

STEP 7: Wrap the neck once or twice.

STEP 8: Trim excess wire if needed.

STEP 9: Hammer the triangle-spiral with a chasing hammer to flatten it (optional).

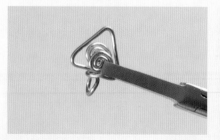

STEP 10: Spiral in the wire end and set it aside. Repeat the above steps until you have 6 to 8 charms for the bracelet.

STEP 11: To make a double-triangle charm, start the same way as for making triangle-spiral charms. Flush cut about 8" (20.3 cm) of 20-gauge wire and create a small spiral. Begin bending sharp angles into the wire as shown.

STEP 12: Bend a second sharp angle.

STEP 13: Bend a third sharp angle.

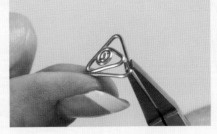

STEP 14: Now bend a fourth angle.

STEP 15: Here is the fifth sharp angle.

STEP 16: The sixth and final angle is shown here.

STEP 17: Bend the wire straight up out of the triangle.

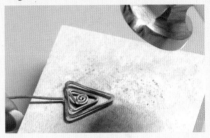

STEP 18: Hammer the triangle with a chasing hammer. Repeat the above steps until you have 6 to 8 charms for the bracelet.

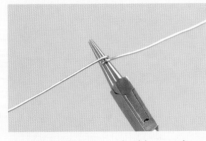

STEP 19: To start a double-spiral charm, flush cut about 6" (15.2 cm) of 20-gauge wire. Grasp the middle of the wire in the middle of the small round-nose pliers and form a loop.

STEP 20: Spiral in each end until they touch.

STEP 21: Grasp the spirals in flat-nose pliers and use chain-nose pliers to bend and twist the loop so that it is at a 90-degree angle to the spirals.

STEP 22: Flatten the spirals with a chasing hammer. Repeat Steps 19–22 until you have 6 to 8 charms for the bracelet.

STEP 23: Make a spiral with a wrapped eye-pin loop with 8" (20.3 cm) of 20-gauge wire. Spiral it in four or five times and then bend the wire straight up out of the spiral. Use round-nose pliers to form an eye-pin loop at the spiral top and wrap the neck as with a bead dangle. Spiral in the wire end.

STEP 24: Tuck the smaller spiral against the bigger one and press down firmly with flat-nose pliers. Repeat Steps 23–24 until you have 6 to 8 charms for the bracelet.

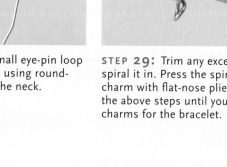

STEP 25: To make a spiraled leaf charm, start with 6" (15.2 cm) of 20-gauge wire. Spiral in one end about three times and then bend a sharp angle into the wire with flat-nose pliers as shown.

STEP 26: Spiral the wire around the outer edge of the charm.

STEP 27: Bend the wire straight up out of the spiral.

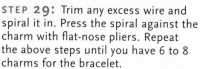

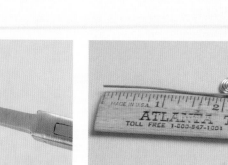

STEP 28: Create a small eye-pin loop at the top of the spiral using round-nose pliers and wrap the neck.

STEP 29: Trim any excess wire and spiral it in. Press the spiral against the charm with flat-nose pliers. Repeat the above steps until you have 6 to 8 charms for the bracelet.

STEP 30: Set all the wire charms aside and begin making the spiral links that form the base for the bracelet. Flush cut eight 18-gauge wire pieces, each 5¼" (13.3 cm) long. Spiral in one end until it's 2¼" (5.7 cm) long; repeat with the remaining wire pieces.

NOTE: Each wire must be exactly the same length. If you have small wrists, you may need only 7 wire links.

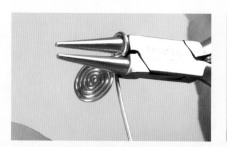

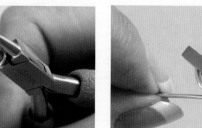

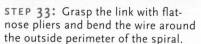

STEP 31: Grasp the wire in the back of the small round-nose pliers and wrap the wire around the tool as shown.

STEP 32: You may need to move the tool in your hand so that you can wrap the wire all the way around it.

STEP 33: Grasp the link with flat-nose pliers and bend the wire around the outside perimeter of the spiral.

STEP 34: Bend the wire straight up out of the spiral.

STEP 35: Open the link sideways and add 1 of each of the bead dangles and 2 to 3 wire charms on it.

STEP 36: Continue placing more charms and beads on the link.

STEP 37: Close the link sideways and press it firmly with flat-nose pliers.

STEP 38: Grasp the link in flat-nose and chain-nose pliers and twist once.

STEP 39: Trim the wire to 1/2" (1.3 cm) long.

STEP 40: Use small round-nose pliers to bend a loop in the straight wire.

STEP 41: Break the neck to center the loop on the link.

STEP 42: Connect the links together. Open the loop you just made and insert it into the closed loop on another link.

STEP 43: Attach a toggle clasp to each end of the bracelet. If necessary, add a small figure-eight or easy link to the bracelet to extend its length.

OPTION: Use a hot solution of liver of sulfur to darken your bracelet (see Basics section pp. 8–19). Polish with 0000 steel wool followed by a jeweler's polishing cloth.

COOL IDEAS!

✳ Raid your scrap pile of leftover wire bits from larger projects to make little wire charms.

✳ This bracelet is beautifully made with copper wire, but other options include sterling silver, gold-filled, craft wire, or yellow brass wire. Or try making it with mixed metals.

✳ Adding just a few small silver and gemstone beads to a predominantly copper bracelet gives it an elegant look.

✳ To keep the toggle from riding on top of your wrist, add a counterweight bead to one end of the bracelet.

PEACOCK WHEELS NECKLACE

RACHEL NELSON-SMITH

Tiny seed beads and sparkly crystals fit nicely onto fine-gauge copper wire. Turning each beaded wire link into the spoke of a wheel results in a stunning necklace any peacock would be proud of.

FINISHED SIZE: *18" (46 cm)*

MATERIALS

85 black AB2 x 4mm Swarovski bicones

85 aquamarine AB2 x 3mm Swarovski bicones

85 turquoise opaque size 11° seed beads

85 blue-gray luster size 11° seed beads

About 7 g copper size 11° seed beads

85 dark blue metallic AB size 8° seed beads

18" (46 cm) of copper dapped bar chain

Toggle clasp

3' (91 cm) of round dead-soft copper 22-gauge wire

1' (31 cm) of round dead-soft copper 20-gauge wire

TOOLS

Flush cutters

0000 steel wool

Small round-nose pliers

Flat-nose pliers

Chain-nose pliers

STEP **1:** Clean your wire thoroughly with 0000 steel wool (see Basics section pp. 8–19). Flush cut (see Basics section pp. 8–19) several pieces of 22-gauge wire, each 1⅛" (2.9 cm) long.

STEP **2:** Bend a small loop in the end of the wire, near the tip of small round-nose pliers.

STEP **3:** Break the neck.

STEP **4:** Center the loop on the straight wire.

STEP **5:** String on 1 black AB2 x 4mm bicone, 1 size 8° seed bead, 1 aquamarine AB2 x 3mm bicone, 1 copper size 11° seed bead, 1 blue size 11° seed bead, and 1 turquoise size 11° seed bead.

STEP **6:** Bend a small loop in the end of the wire, near the tip of small round-nose pliers.

STEP **7:** Break the neck.

STEP **8:** Repeat from Step 1 until you have 17 beaded wire eye-pin links.

STEP **9:** String one end of each link onto a 4" (10 cm) piece of 22-gauge wire. Shape the wire into a circle.

STEP **10:** Trim the wire ends.

STEP **11:** Place the wheel of links onto a tabletop and fan out the "spokes" of the wheel.

STEP **12:** Cut a 1' (30.5 cm) long piece of 22-gauge wire and string one end through an eye-pin loop on the end of one beaded link. Add 4 size 11° copper beads, and then run the wire through the next eye-pin loop.

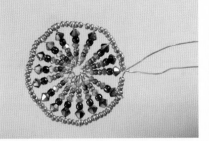

STEP 13: Continue stringing on beads as in Step 12.

STEP 14: Bring both wire ends through the final eye-pin loop.

STEP 15: Bring both wires up together and place them on the round-nose pliers near the tip. Wrap the wire around the pliers in a loop.

STEP 16: Trim the wire ends.

STEP 17: Press down the wire ends.

STEP 18: Create several small 20-gauge jump rings and use them to attach the wheels to a commercial necklace chain.

STEP 19: Make 5 Peacock Wheels and attach them to the center of the chain, about 1" (3 cm) apart. Add a clasp to finish.

COOL IDEAS!

⁎ Try making wheels with different colored beads, crystals, and small pearls to vary the look.

⁎ This necklace also looks great when made with sterling silver or gold-filled wire or even colored craft wire.

⁎ Try making wheels with a much larger circumference by cutting longer lengths of wire for each spoke and adding more beads.

found PEBBLES NecklaCe

RICHARD SALLEY

Have you ever picked up a handful of pebbles and wished you could turn them into jewelry? Artist Richard Salley shows you how to use dark annealed steel wire to turn your found pebbles into beads without holes, and make them into a funky piece of wearable art.

FINISHED SIZE: $16^1/_2$" (41.9 cm)

MATERIALS

4 pebbles about 32x13mm
1 pebble about 45x19mm
3' (91 cm) of round dark annealed steel 19-gauge wire
3' (91 cm) of round dark annealed steel 16-gauge wire

TOOLS

Jewelry file
Measuring tape
0000 steel wool
Indelible marker
Small steel bench block
Hardware store wire cutters
Small round-nose pliers
Flat-nose pliers
Chain-nose pliers
Bail-forming pliers

STEP 1: Clean all the wire thoroughly with 0000 steel wool (see Basics section pp. 8–19). Clean the pebbles as well if necessary with soap and water.

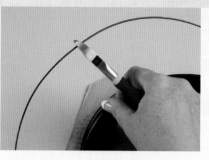

STEP 2: Cut six to eight 6" (15 cm) pieces of 19-gauge steel wire using heavy-duty wire cutters. File the ends if necessary and set them aside.

STEP 3: Wrap about 1' (30 cm) of 16-gauge steel wire around a large bail-forming pliers to create a coil.

STEP 4: Flush cut the coil (see Basics section).

STEP 5: Cut off a ring, making sure that both ends of the ring are flush cut.

STEP 6: Make 34 jump rings this way and set them aside.

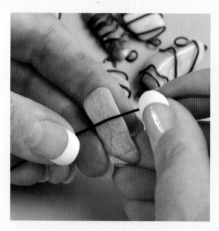

STEP 7: Grasping 1 wire piece from Step 2, place a pebble on its center.

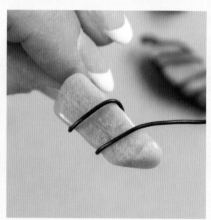

STEP 8: Wrap the wire around it, pressing firmly.

Continue wrapping the wire around the pebble until you have about 1/2" (1.3 cm) of straight wire remaining on each end.

STEP 9: Use round-nose pliers to create a small eye-pin loop with the straight wire ends.

OPTION: Hammer the eye-pin loops with a chasing or planishing hammer.

STEP 10: Use flat-nose pliers to twist the wire slightly, which tightens the wire wrap on the pebble and gives it a decorative touch.

STEP 11: Use a jump ring to connect 2 of the smaller wire-wrapped pebbles together. Repeat for a second length of linked pebbles. Set them aside.

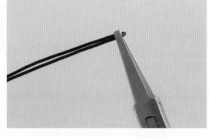

STEP 12: To wrap a larger pebble or stone for the necklace's focal bead, cut a 10" (25 cm) piece of 16-gauge or 19-gauge steel wire. File the wire ends if necessary. Fold the wire in half.

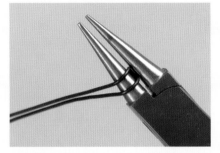

STEP 13: Bend the wire with the small round-nose pliers to create a small hook.

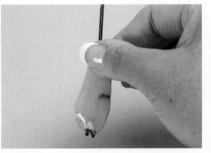

STEP 14: Wrap the wire around the back of the stone.

STEP 15: Separate the 2 wires at the top of the stone and press the wire firmly against it.

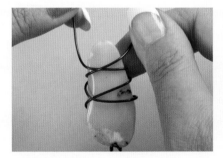

STEP 16: Continue wrapping the wire around the stone.

STEP 17: Use flat-nose pliers to twist the wire tight around the stone.

COOL IDEAS!

* To prevent rust, spray the wire (before making jewelry with it) with a matte acrylic spray.

* Adjust the necklace length by adding or subtracting wire-wrapped pebbles or jump rings.

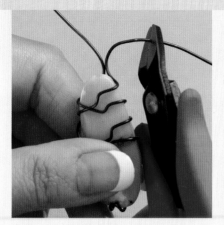

STEP 18: Trim the wire ends.

STEP 19: Bend the wire ends in round loops.

STEP 20: Use jump rings to connect the large pendant stone to the 2 lengths of linked pebbles.

STEP 21: Add more jump rings to each end of the necklace to desired length.

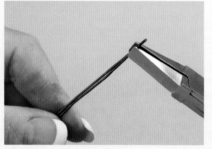

STEP 22: Flush cut a 4" (10 cm) long piece of 16-gauge wire and bend it in half.

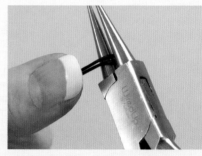

STEP 23: Bend the wire with round-nose pliers to create a small hook.

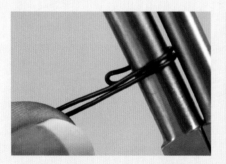

STEP 24: Bend the wire hook over in a pair of large bail-forming pliers.

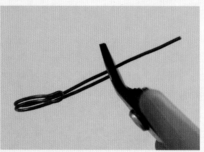

STEP 25: Trim the wire ends if needed.

STEP 26: Bend loops in the wire ends on the round-nose pliers.

STEP 27: The finished hook.

STEP 28: Attach the hook to the necklace.

STEP 29: The back of the finished necklace.

FUNKY chandelier Earrings

SHARILYN MILLER

These swing-style chandelier earrings are a bit chunky due to the large turquoise beads and carnelians used to fashion them. For a more elegant statement, try making these earrings with your favorite sparkly crystals and pearls.

FINISHED SIZE: 2 ³/8" (6 cm)

MATERIALS

6 turquoise 12mm rondelles

4 carnelian 8mm rondelles

4 light green 5mm glass rondelles

8 copper 5mm discs

8 copper 4mm rounds

4 silver 3mm cornerless cubes

12" (30.5 cm) of round dead-soft copper 22-gauge wire

4" (10.1 cm) of round dead-soft copper 20-gauge wire

4" (10.1 cm) of round dead-soft sterling silver 18-gauge wire

18" (46 cm) of annealed steel 24-, 26- or 28-gauge wire

TOOLS

Flush cutters

Measuring tape

0000 steel wool

Small jeweler's bench block

Chasing or planishing hammer

Small round-nose pliers

Large round-nose pliers

Flat-nose pliers

Chain-nose pliers

STEP 1: Clean the wire thoroughly with 0000 steel wool. Flush cut 2 pieces of 22-gauge wire, each piece 6" (15 cm) long. Use small round-nose pliers to create a double-wrapped eye-pin loop on one end of each wire piece. String beads and spacer beads onto each wire piece in your order of preference.

STEP 2: Use small round-nose pliers to create a double-wrapped eye-pin loop on the opposite end of each wire piece to finish.

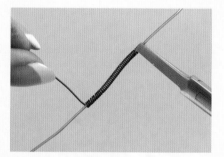

STEP 3: Bend the bead-strung wires into U shapes and set them aside.

STEP 4: Coil wrap fine-gauge wire (24-gauge, 26-gauge, or 28-gauge) onto 20-gauge wire until you have a coil about 2" (5.1 cm) long.

STEP 5: Remove the coil and flush cut it so that you have 2 coils, each about 1" (2.54 cm) long.

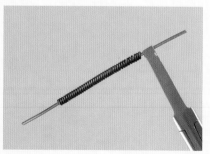

STEP 6: Flush cut the coil ends.

STEP 7: Flush cut 2 pieces of 20-gauge wire, each about 2" (5.1 cm) long. Place a coil onto each wire piece.

STEP 8: Make simple (unwrapped) eye-pin loops on each wire end.

STEP 9: Bend the two coil-wrapped wires into U shapes.

STEP 10: Open each eye-pin loop from the previous steps and use them to attach to the bead-strung wires. Set these aside.

STEP 11: Flush cut 2 pieces of 20-gauge wire (sterling silver recommended), each about 2" (5.1 cm) long. Create French ear wires as described in the Basics section, but before wrapping each eye-pin loop, open it sideways and place a coil-wrapped wire inside it to permanently attach the ear wire to the dangle created earlier.

STEP 12: Wrap the wire beneath each eye-pin loop and trim or spiral the wire end. Bend the wire forward as shown.

STEP 13: Use large round-nose pliers to shape ear wires.

OPTION: Forge the ear wires with a chasing hammer as desired. Be sure to file the wire ends using a flat file or a cup burr to make them smooth.

COOL IDEAS!

✳ Look for small, lightweight beads and spacers to use in your earring designs because they won't drag on your earlobes.

✳ As in any jewelry piece, the beads you use in these earrings will determine their style. For a bold, ethnic look, use big turquoise chunks, carnelian or amber, and metal beads as shown in the sample. For a more elegant design, use sparkly crystals, pearls, and fancy handmade glass beads.

✳ Substitute sterling silver or gold-filled wire for copper and annealed steel wire to create a more high-end fashion statement.

✳ For ear wires, I recommend using sterling silver or gold-filled wire because some people are sensitive to copper and other metals in their earlobes.

✳ Before making several earring pairs, start coiling fine-gauge wire (24-gauge, 26-gauge, 28-gauge) onto heavier gauge wire such as 20-gauge. Create long coils and place them in your bead box, ready to cut into short segments for use in future earring designs.

COIN-PEARL
COPPER-WASHER BRACELET

SHARILYN MILLER

Large copper washers from the hardware store frame big coin pearls in this mixed-metals bracelet designed with a handmade toggle clasp.

FINISHED SIZE: *8" (20.3 cm)*

MATERIALS

1 copper ³/₄" (19mm) washer
6 copper 1" (25mm) washers
6 blue 13mm coin pearls
3' (91 cm) of round dead-soft sterling silver 22-gauge wire
2' (61 cm) of round dead-soft sterling silver 18-gauge wire

TOOLS

Flush cutters
Measuring tape
0000 steel wool
Hard-plastic mallet
Small embossing hammer
Small jeweler's bench block
Small round-nose pliers
Large round-nose pliers
Flat-nose pliers
Chain-nose pliers

STEP 1: Clean all the wire thoroughly with oooo steel wool (see Basics section pp. 8–19) and set it aside. Use the large end of a small embossing hammer to texture one side of each copper washer. Then use the small end of a small embossing hammer to texture the outer edge of each copper washer.

STEP 2: Flush cut (see Basics section pp. 8–19) 22-gauge wire into 6" (15.2 cm) lengths, one for each coin pearl in the bracelet.

STEP 3: Run a 22-gauge wire piece through a coin pearl and bring the pearl to the center of the wire. Then lay the coin pearl on top of a large textured copper washer, with the textured pattern upright.

STEP 4: Wrap the wire around the washer as shown.

STEP 5: Start by wrapping one time, then go to the other side and wrap that wire once, and then continue wrapping both wires until you have wrapped the washer three times on both sides.

STEP 6: Use the remaining wire ends to wrap around the "necks" on both sides, as shown.

STEP 7: Wrap about two or three times. Bring both wires to the textured side of the washer and trim as needed so they each measure ¹/₂" (1.3 cm) long. Use the tips of the small round-nose pliers followed by flat-nose pliers to create tiny spirals with each wire end. Tuck them firmly against the coin pearl. Repeat from Step 3 for each coin pearl.

STEP 8: Flush cut 14 pieces of 18-gauge wire, each piece 1³/₈" (3.5 cm) long. Use the wire pieces to form figure-eight links on the back of the small round-nose pliers.

STEP 9: Use a hard-plastic mallet to hammer each figure eight on the bench block to work-harden them (see Basics section pp. 8–19). Connect coin pearls framed with copper washers by using doubled figure-eight links.

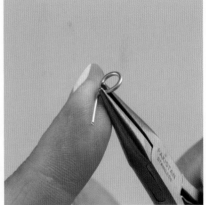

STEP 10: Here is how the pattern should look.

STEP 11: Use 1¹/₂" (3.8 cm) of 18-gauge wire to create a small easy link.

STEP 12: Break the neck.

coin-pearl copper-washer bracelet   43

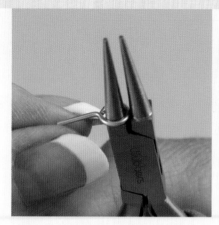

STEP 13: Reinsert the round-nose pliers and center the loop on the straight wire.

STEP 14: Make a tiny loop in the middle of the small round-nose pliers.

STEP 15: Break the neck.

STEP 16: A finished easy link.

STEP 17: Attach an easy link to one end of the bracelet. Set the bracelet aside.

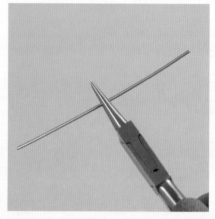

STEP 18: To form the bar end of a toggle clasp, flush cut 2¹⁄₂" (6.4 cm) of 18-gauge wire. Grasp the wire in the middle with round-nose pliers.

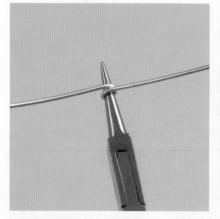

STEP 19: Form a small loop in the middle of small round-nose pliers.

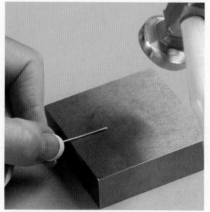

STEP 20: Flatten the ends with a chasing hammer.

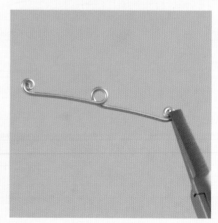

STEP 21: Spiral them in.

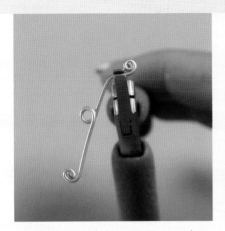

STEP 22: Bend the wire in a toggle shape on the small flat-nose pliers.

STEP 23: Attach the finished toggle to the bracelet and try it on for fit. Additional coin pearls framed with copper washers may need to be added to the bracelet, depending on your wrist size.

COOL IDEAS!

✳ I recommend using a hot solution of liver of sulfur to darken and "artificially age" the metal (see Basics section pp. 8–19). The antique look is especially effective when making jewelry with mixed metals.

✳ Coin pearls are available in various sizes. For this bracelet, I went for a bold, ethnic look using ½" (1.3 cm) diameter coin pearls. Therefore, I had to use the largest size copper washers in my collection to frame the pearls. If you wish, you can make a more delicate bracelet using smaller coin pearls and washers.

✳ Always test your coin pearls and washers for fit before wiring the pearls in place. Place a washer on a tabletop and then place a coin pearl inside. There should be at least ⅛" (.32 cm) clearance between the outside edge of the pearl and the inside edge of the washer, allowing room for the doubled figure-eight links that will be attached later.

WiRE-WOVEN PENDANT

EUGENIA CHAN

A handmade bead with a very large hole is the ideal choice for this pendant fashioned with a wire-woven bead cap. Rubber cording or a similar material makes the necklace surprisingly economical.

FINISHED SIZE: *22" (56 cm)*

MATERIALS

Bead cap (optional)

5' (152 cm) of rubber cording

1 stone bead about 25 x 45mm with a hole that accommodates five 20-gauge wires

5' (2 m) of round dead-soft copper 20-gauge wire

5' (2 m) of round dead-soft copper 24-gauge wire

TOOLS

Flush cutter

Indelible pen

0000 steel wool

Chasing hammer

Small steel bench block

Small round-nose pliers

Flat-nose pliers

Chain-nose pliers

Bail-forming pliers

STEP 1: Clean all of the wire thoroughly with 0000 steel wool (see Basics section pp. 8–19). Flush cut (see Basics section) 5 pieces of 20-gauge wire, each about 8" (20 cm) long. One by one, start a spiral at one end of each wire using the tips of the small round-nose pliers.

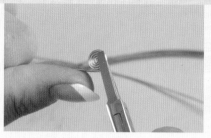

STEP 2: Use flat-nose pliers to spiral the wire for about 1–1½" (3–4 cm). Repeat with the remaining 4 wire pieces.

STEP 3: Hammer the spirals lightly with a chasing hammer.

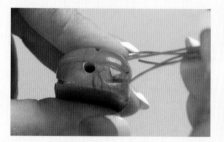

STEP 4: Test the wires on your large focal bead; all 5 must pass through the hole simultaneously.

STEP 5: Run all 5 wires through the bead cap (optional) and then through the bead.

STEP 6: Pull the wires through snugly.

STEP 7: Use large bail-forming pliers to wrap an eye-pin loop (see Basics section) in the wire just above the bead.

STEP 8: Use chain-nose pliers to break the neck.

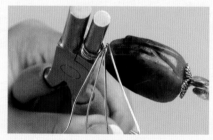

Begin wrapping the neck. Once you've wrapped all 5 wires around once or twice, begin to separate them.

OPTION: If you wish to use a bead cap on the bottom of the pendant, test the hole. As with the bead, all 5 wires must pass through the bead cap simultaneously.

STEP 9: Try to separate each wire equally, like the spokes on a wheel. Set the bead aside.

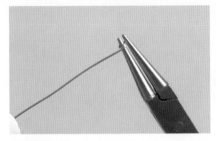

STEP 10: Cut 5' (2 m) of 24-gauge sterling silver wire and create a tiny loop on one end.

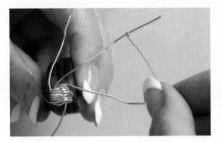

STEP 11: Place this loop on one of the wire "spokes." Slide it all the way down until it sits next to the bead.

STEP 12: Begin wrapping the 24-gauge wire once around each spoke, moving in a clockwise direction.

STEP 13: Wrap around several rotations to create a basket-woven bead cap on the focal bead.

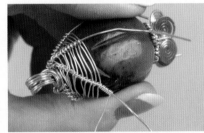

STEP 14: After going around about a dozen times, stop on one spoke and simply wrap the wire around it to form a coil.

STEP 15: When the coil is about 1½"–1¾" (4–5 cm) long, trim the excess wire with flush cutters.

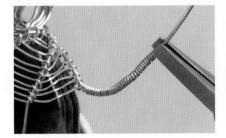

STEP 16: Press the cut wire firmly against the spoke.

STEP 17: Spiral in the spoke, starting with round-nose pliers and finishing with flat-nose pliers. Note how loose and open the spiral is.

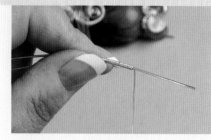

STEP 18: Coil the remaining 24-gauge wire onto a 20-gauge wire mandrel. Remove the coil.

STEP 19: Cut the coil in half and then both halves in half again. Flush cut the ends.

STEP 20: Place a coil onto each spoke, pushing it all the way up.

STEP 21: Spiral in all the wires and tuck them against the focal bead. Turn and twist the spirals protruding from the bottom of the focal bead so they lay nicely.

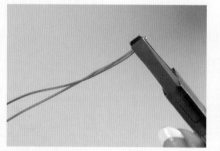

STEP 22: To make a hook clasp, flush cut a 12" (31 cm) piece of 20-gauge wire and fold it in half with flat-nose pliers.

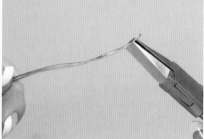

STEP 23: Press the wires together firmly.

STEP 24: Bend the wire into a hook in the back of the round-nose pliers.

STEP 25: Switch to bail-forming pliers. Turn the hook over, facing you, and place it in the pliers. Roll the wire over until you have formed a shepherd's hook.

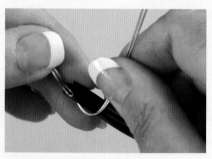

Cut the rubber cording in half and fold both pieces in half. Holding the four cut ends together, wrap the wire from the hook clasp around the rubber cording.

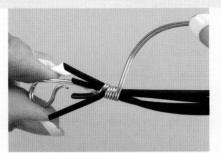

STEP 26: Wrap several times around the cording tightly to secure it.

STEP 27: Trim away any excess cording.

STEP 28: Wrap the wire over the cut ends of the rubber cording.

STEP 29: Spiral in each wire end and press it against the wrapped wire using flat-nose pliers.

STEP 30: This is how the hook clasp should look. Run the folded rubber cording through the wrapped eye-pin loop on the pendant and then secure it with the wire hook.

COOL IDEAS!

✳ This necklace can be made of varying lengths by using more or less cording and fewer metal components.

✳ If you'd rather not immerse the cording in liver of sulfur, artificially age the metal components in this solution first and then polish them before assembling the necklace.

✳ If you prefer to tumble polish your jewelry, tumble the individual components first and then assemble them on a necklace with cording.

forged paddle earrings

SHARILYN MILLER

Forged wire "paddles" made of short lengths of 12-gauge wire are easily made into lightweight, fun-to-wear earring dangles.

FINISHED SIZE: 2 3/4" (7 cm)

MATERIALS

3" (7.6 cm) of round dead-soft copper 12-gauge wire

4" (10.1 cm) of round dead-soft sterling silver 22-gauge wire

6" (15.2 cm) of round dead-soft sterling silver 20-gauge wire

TOOLS

Indelible pen

Flush cutters

0000 steel wool

Small jeweler's flat file

Small steel bench block

Small metal hole punch

Small embossing hammer

Chasing or planishing hammer

Hard-plastic or rawhide mallet

Small round-nose pliers

Large round-nose pliers

Flat-nose pliers

Chain-nose pliers

STEP 1: Clean your wire thoroughly with oooo steel wool (see Basics section pp. 8–19). Flush cut (Basics section) the wire end.

STEP 2: Flush cut a piece of wire about 1¹⁄₂" (3.8 cm) long.

STEP 3: Repeat these first two steps to create wire pieces of equal length.

STEP 4: Forge one end of each wire piece with a chasing or planishing hammer to thin down the end just a little bit; don't overdo this step.

STEP 5: File the edges with a small flat file to smooth them.

STEP 6: Use a small embossing hammer to forge texture into the paddle area of the wire. Start with the larger head of the hammer and then switch to the smaller head and texture around the edges of the paddle. Repeat Steps 3–6 with the second wire piece.

 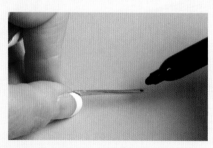 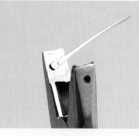

STEP 7: Turn one of the wires one-half turn on the bench block and forge the opposite end, hammering firmly several times with a chasing or planishing hammer to flatten the wire into a wide, long paddle. Repeat with the second wire piece, ensuring that they are similar in size and length to each other.

STEP 8: Use an indelible pen to mark the wire about ¹⁄₈" (.32 cm) from the edge of each wire piece.

STEP 9: Use a small metal hole punch to punch a hole right at the mark on both wires.

STEP 10: This is what the wire end should look like, with a small hole nicely centered.

STEP 11: Flush cut 2 pieces of 22-gauge sterling silver wire, each about 2" (5.1 cm) long.

STEP 12: Wrap each piece around a copper paddle, near the end with a punched hole.

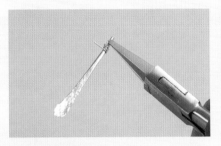

STEP 13: Wrap around three times and then spiral in the ends. Press the wire and spirals firmly against the copper paddles using flat-nose pliers. Repeat with the other paddle.

STEP 14: Flush cut 2 pieces of 20-gauge or 22-gauge sterling silver wire, each about 3" (7.6 cm) long.

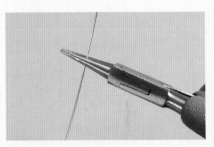

STEP 15: Grasp the wire in the middle of the round-nose pliers.

STEP 16: Bring the wire around the tool.

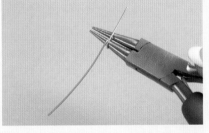

STEP 17: The wire is wrapped all the way around the tool one complete time.

STEP 18: Remove the round-nose pliers and insert the tip of the chain-nose pliers into the loop.

STEP 19: Bend the wire back at a sharp angle.

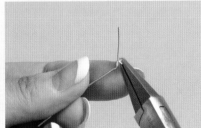

STEP 20: Open the loop sideways.

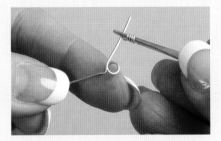

STEP 21: Insert the short wire end through the punched hole in one of the hammered wire pieces.

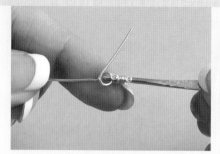

STEP 22: Close the loop with chain-nose pliers.

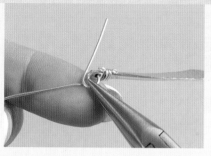

STEP 23: Repeat Steps 15–22 with the second wire piece.

STEP 24: Begin wrapping the neck.

STEP 25: Continue wrapping the neck.

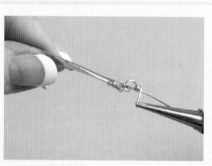

STEP 26: Begin a tiny spiral on the end of the wire.

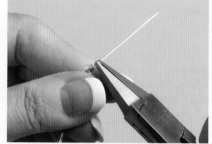

STEP 27: Press it tight with the tips of the flat-nose pliers.

STEP 28: Here is how it should look at this point.

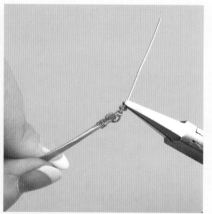

STEP 29: Bend the wire forward, over the spiral.

STEP 30: Bend the wire up and over one of the jaws of the large bail-forming pliers.

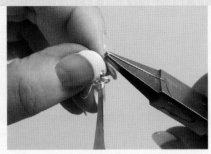

STEP 31: Take hold of the wire end in the tips of the flat-nose pliers.

STEP 32: Bend the wire back at a slight angle.

STEP 33: Forge the ear wire lightly with a chasing hammer.

STEP 34: Use a small flat file to smooth all the edges of each wire piece, paying special attention to the corners. Repeat Steps 25–34 to finish the second earring.

OPTION: Use a hot solution of liver of sulfur to darken your Paddle earrings (see Basics section pp. 8–19). Polish with 0000 steel wool followed by a jeweler's polishing cloth.

COOL IDEAS!

✴ These earrings are easy to make, but they do require some effort to make them well. Take time when forging the copper wire pieces, making them as similar in appearance as possible. You may have to create three or more paddles before you find that two of them are similar enough to make a matched pair for earrings.

✴ Take care not to over-forge the wire pieces because the wire will become brittle and may crack around the edges.

✴ Paddles do not have to be textured; they look very nice as smooth metal dangles, too.

✴ Make smaller (shorter) paddles and use them as dangles for charm bracelets and necklaces.

✴ Take time when filing the wire edges to make them very smooth to avoid scratching your skin and to keep the metal from catching on clothing. Feel the edges and corners with your fingertip to ensure that they not only look smooth but actually are smooth; your eyes may lie, but your fingertips never will.

COIN-PEARL COIL-WRAPPED BRACELET

SHARILYN MILLER

Flat coin pearls and diamond-shaped pearls are framed with delicate coil-wrapped wire in this mixed-metals bracelet.

FINISHED SIZE: 8" *(20.3 cm)*

MATERIALS

1 toggle clasp
1 head pin with decorative head
1 silver 6mm faceted rondelle
1 silver 12mm heart-shaped bead
7 green-gold 12mm coin pearls
7' (213 cm) of round dead-soft copper 24-gauge wire
3' (91 cm) of round dead-soft sterling silver 22-gauge wire
3' (91 cm) of round dead-soft sterling silver 20-gauge wire
1' (31 cm) of round dead-soft copper 16-gauge wire

TOOLS

Flush cutters
Measuring tape
0000 steel wool
Small round-nose pliers
Flat-nose pliers
Chain-nose pliers

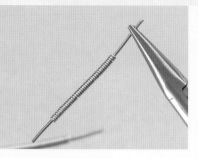

STEP 1: Clean all of your wire with 0000 steel wool (see Basics section pp. 8–19). Coil the 24-gauge copper wire onto 20-gauge sterling silver wire. Remove the coil from the 20-gauge wire and flush cut the coil into segments, each 7/8" (2.2 cm) long.

STEP 2: Flush cut (see Basics section pp. 8–19) 20-gauge silver wire into 14 pieces, each 1 5/8" (4.1 cm) long.

STEP 3: Place a coil from the previous step onto each of these wire pieces. Bring the coil to the exact center of each wire piece.

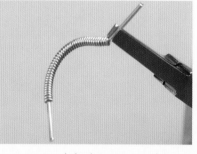

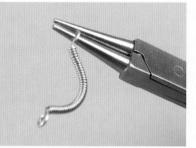

STEP 4: Bend the coil-wrapped wire around the edge of a coin pearl to see if it will fit.

STEP 5: Bend the bare wire ends at a sharp angle to the rounded bent and coiled wire.

STEP 6: Use small round-nose pliers to form tiny eye-pin loops at each end.

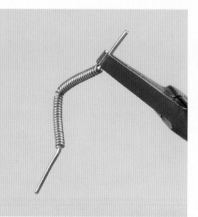

STEP 7: OPTION: If using diamond-shaped instead of coin-shaped pearls, bend the wire at a 90-degree angle.

STEP 8: Bend the bare wire ends at a sharp angle to the bent and coiled wire. Create eye-pin loops as indicated in the previous steps.

STEP 9: Run 4" (10 cm) of 22-gauge sterling silver wire through each pearl and create small eye-pin loops on each end. Set these pieces aside.

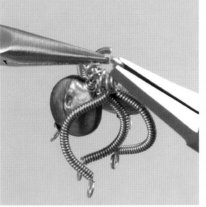

STEP 10: On the back of the small round-nose pliers, form 7 jump rings using 16-gauge copper wire. Use these jump rings to connect the coin-pearl connectors and their frames of coil-wrapped wire. Note that you may need more or fewer of these units, depending on your wrist size.

STEP 11: Here you see 2 units being joined together: 2 coin-pearl connectors, each framed by coil-wrapped wire.

STEP 12: Here is a view of how the bracelet is laid out and connected with jump rings.

STEP 13: On each end of the bracelet, attach a toggle clasp using either jump rings or small wire links.

OPTION: Artificially aging this bracelet in hot liver of sulfur is recommended (see Basics section pp. 8–19). Whenever applying this process to a jewelry piece with pearls, dip the piece in the solution quickly and remove it as soon as the wire has turned to the desired color. Then rinse the jewelry in cool water immediately to protect the pearls.

COOL IDEAS!

✳ Accurate wire measurements are the key to good results with this bracelet design. That being said, if your tools are different and the beads you use are of different measurements than the ones used in the sample bracelet, you will need to make changes accordingly. For instance, a coin pearl with a 3/4" diameter will require larger coil-wrapped wire frames than the one shown here, which will in turn require more wire.

✳ Because this is a very lightweight bracelet, attaching a counter-weight bead near the clasp is a good idea.

✳ The design of this bracelet is easy to alter by using different wire colors and beads of various shapes and sizes. As you experiment, be sure to note the changes you make and any alterations made to the wire measurements used, because these details are easy to forget.

elemental necklace
DALE "COUGAR" ARMSTRONG

Well-known jewelry designer and teacher Dale "Cougar" Armstrong sent us a beautiful necklace made with sterling silver wire, large crystals without holes, and small silver and garnet beads. Using her design and instructions, I made a similar necklace using dark annealed steel and copper wires plus natural-colored agates and other beads. While my necklace looks very different from Dale's, the original design is all her own.

FINISHED SIZE: 23" (58 cm)

MATERIALS

1 toggle clasp

About 50 copper head pins, each 3" (8 cm) long

About 100–150 beads: wide variety of large agate chips, small gemstones, spacer beads, and metal beads

3' (91 cm) of round dark annealed steel 16-gauge wire

10' (254 cm) of round dead-soft copper 22-gauge wire

3' (1 m) of round dark annealed steel 19-gauge wire

10' (3 m) of round dead-soft copper 22-gauge wire

TOOLS

Flush cutters

Measuring tape

0000 steel wool

Chasing or planishing hammer

Hard-plastic or rawhide mallet

Large (4" x 4") (10 x 10 cm) jeweler's bench block

Small round-nose pliers

Flat-nose pliers

Chain-nose pliers

Bail-forming pliers

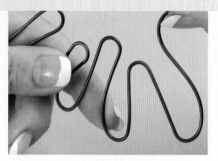

STEP 1: Clean the wire thoroughly with 0000 steel wool (see Basics section pp. 8–19). Flush cut (see Basics section) about 2'–3' (61–91 cm) of 16-gauge dark annealed steel wire (copper or yellow brass wire may be substituted) and begin to bend it into rounded shapes.

STEP 2: Use various tools such as round-nose pliers and bail-forming pliers to shape the wire.

STEP 3: Use round-nose pliers to bend large round eye-pin loops on each end of the wire framework.

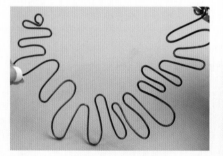

STEP 4: Here is the finished necklace frame; feel free to make changes and bend the wire in different ways to your satisfaction.

STEP 5: Use a hard-plastic or rawhide mallet to hammer the necklace frame on a 4" x 4" (10 x 10 cm) steel bench block. This work-hardens (see Basics section pp. 8–19) the wire and causes it to hold its shape.

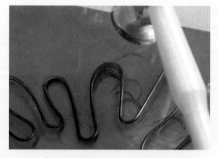

STEP 6: Switch to a chasing or planishing hammer to forge the rounded bends in the wire. This makes the finished necklace frame permanent and provides more design area upon which to attach beads and other decorative elements.

STEP 7: Organize your beads into color groups and divide them according to size and shape. Use large agate chips, small gemstones, and small metal beads in your design to create texture and variety.

STEP 8: It helps to lay everything out on your worktable where you can see all of your materials easily. Once you have everything well organized, place the wire frame in front of you and place your largest beads or chips on it in a design pattern.

STEP 9: Here you can see how I have arranged large agate chips on the frame in a colorful pattern with plenty of variety. Set this aside for the moment.

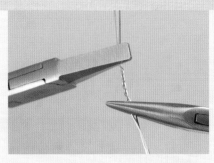

STEP 10: Flush cut two 8" (20 cm) pieces of 20-gauge wire and twist them together a few times near one end, leaving about 3" (8 cm) of straight wire extending beyond the twist on one end.

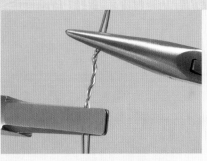

STEP 11: Repeat this step on the opposite end of the wires, leaving a gap between the twists about 1/2"–1" (1.3–3 cm) long.

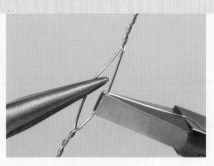

STEP 12: Gently pull apart the straight wires in the middle.

STEP 13: Place an agate chip (or large bead of your choice) into the gap. If the gap is too large to fit the bead, twist the wire until it fits tightly.

STEP 14: Press the wires against the bead and twist a few times on each side. Then bring 2 wires in front of the bead and 2 wires behind it. Begin to twist them together.

STEP 15: Here is another view of the wires twisted together at the top of the bead.

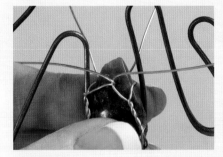

STEP 16: Place the wire-wrapped bead on the necklace frame and prepare to make the attachment.

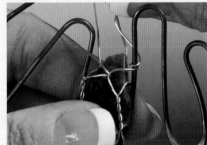

STEP 17: Hold the bead firmly in place on the frame as you wrap the copper wires around the frame, attaching the bead.

STEP 18: After coiling the copper wire onto the frame, press the ends down firmly with the tips of chain-nose pliers.

elemental necklace   65

STEP **19:** Another way to finish the wire ends is to spiral them in and press them firmly against the wire frame.

NOTE: These next few steps are optional and useful for covering up the hole drilled through agate chips.

STEP **20:** Pick up a 3" (8 cm) copper head pin and string on a couple of small metal beads.

STEP **21:** Run the head pin through the hole in the chip as shown.

STEP **22:** Wrap the head-pin wire around the necklace frame to securely attach the agate in place.

STEP **23:** Flush cut a piece of 22-gauge or 20-gauge copper wire about 8"–10" (20–25 cm) long and begin wrapping it around the necklace frame. String on a few beads, gemstones, and spacers at a time and wrap them in place.

STEP **24:** Continue wrapping the wire around the frame to hold everything securely. When you run out of wire, spiral on the ends; the spirals become an element of the design.

STEP **25:** Continue attaching large agate chips, small gemstones, metal beads, and spacer beads with copper wire lengths. You can see the pattern beginning to emerge.

STEP **26:** As you work on the necklace, feel the back side for rough edges of beads or cut wire that should be filed or pressed firmly against the frame to keep the necklace from scratching the wearer.

STEP **27:** Fill the necklace with as many beads as you choose but always be sure to finish off the wire ends.

STEP 28: Extra-long lengths of wire may be trimmed as necessary.

STEP 29: Spiral in the wire ends.

STEP 30: Press the spirals firmly against the wire frame.

STEP 31: Flush cut 2 copper chain pieces to your desired length.

STEP 32: Attach 1 chain to each eye-pin loop on the wire frame by opening the loop sideways.

STEP 33: Close the eye-pin loop securely.

STEP 34: Tighten the eye-pin loop if necessary.

COOL IDEAS!

✳ Try making this necklace with different types of wire: copper, sterling silver, or colored craft wire.

✳ To "glam it up," use crystals, pearls, and brightly colored glass beads instead of the natural stones used in the sample.

✳ Use the techniques shown in this chapter to make necklaces of varying lengths or change the framework pattern to create new shapes.

✳ Before attaching beads to the framework, stand in front of a mirror and hold the piece up to your body where you think it will hang. If the design is too large or too small, unbalanced, etc., you will be able to make adjustments to the frame before attaching any beads to it.

✳ Try using this technique to make a bracelet. Instead of hammering the frame on a flat bench block, hammer it on a metal bracelet mandrel. After checking it for fit, attach beads as described above.

STEP 35: Attach a purchased toggle clasp.

eMBeLLISHED COPPER-WASHER EaRRiNGS

SHARILYN MILLER

A little hammered texturing and a couple of holes transform these ordinary copper washers into great jewelry components for funky earrings.

FINISHED SIZE: 1 7/8" (4.8 cm)

MATERIALS

2 copper 3/4" (1.9 cm) washers

4 metal 4–5mm spacers

4 gemstone or pearl 4–6mm beads

6" (15.2 cm) of round dead-soft sterling silver 22-gauge wire

6 sterling silver 2" (5.1 cm) head pins, 4 with decorative heads

TOOLS

Ruler

Flat file

Flush cutters

Indelible marker

0000 steel wool

Chasing hammer

Small metal hole punch

Small embossing hammer

Small jeweler's bench block

Small round-nose pliers

Large round-nose pliers

Flat-nose pliers

Chain-nose pliers

STEP 1: Use the ball-peen end of a chasing hammer or a small embossing hammer to forge one side of each copper washer on a bench block. This will create surface texture and add interest to these components.

STEP 2: Use the fine tip on the small embossing hammer to create tiny dimples on the outer edges of the copper washers.

STEP 3: Turn the washers over exposing their plain sides and use an indelible marker to draw three dots as shown.

STEP 4: Using these marks as a guide, punch small holes using a small metal hole punch.

STEP 5: It may be necessary to use flat-nose pliers to remove the washer from the small metal hole punch. Set the washers aside.

STEP 6: String a single metal spacer of your choice onto each of the 4 head pins with decorative heads. One by one, run each head pin through a punched hole.

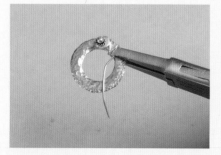  

STEP 7: Wrap the remaining wire around the washer twice, leaving a tail. Repeat so that each washer has 2 wire-wrapped head pins attached.

STEP 8: Use round-nose and flat-nose pliers to tightly spiral the wire tails and press them firmly against each washer. Set them aside.

STEP 9: Use the 2 remaining head pins and 4 small beads or pearls of your choice to create bead dangles with single-wrapped eye-pin loops (see Basics section pp. 8–19).

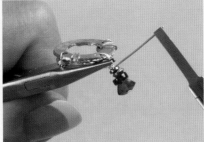

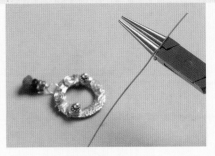

STEP 10: Before wrapping the loops, open them sideways and insert the wire into the hole punched at the bottom of each copper washer.

STEP 11: Close the loop and wrap the neck tightly, spiraling in the wire end as desired.

STEP 12: Clean the 22-gauge wire piece using 0000 steel wool (see Basics section) and flush cut (see Basics section) it into two 3" (7.6 cm) pieces. With one piece, create a round loop starting 1" (2.5 cm) down the wire with the small round-nose pliers.

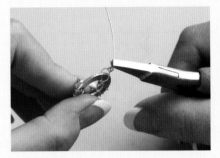

STEP 13: Break the neck and then open the loop sideways. Insert the top of an embellished copper washer into this loop.

STEP 14: Close the loop sideways and wrap the neck tightly, spiraling in the wire end as desired. Repeat with the second piece of wire and embellished copper washer.

STEP 15: Pick up 1 wire and place it in the flat-nose pliers. Bend it forward as shown. Repeat with the second wire piece attached to an embellished copper washer.

STEP 16: Hold the wire piece so the bent end is pointed toward you. Place the wire in the back of the extra-long round-nose pliers and bend the wire up and over to create a shepherd's-hook earring. Repeat with the second earring. As with all ear hooks, bend up the wire ends slightly, using flat-nose pliers. File the wire ends to smooth and round their edges or use a cup burr in a small handheld drill to achieve the same purpose.

COOL IDEAS!

✳ Any type of small gemstone, pearl or metal bead will work for this earring design. Be sure to test the bead holes to ensure that the head pins will pass through them.

✳ Using liver of sulfur to artificially age the finished earrings is a nice finishing touch (see Basics section pp. 8–19). Polish the earrings carefully afterward with 0000 steel wool and jewelry polishing cloths.

✳ Shepherd's-hook-style ear wires can be made using copper, silver, or the metal of your choice.

✳ Head pins can be made of copper or silver; copper will be significantly less expensive.

embellished copper-washer earrings   71

ARTSY FIBULA PIN

EUGENIA CHAN

Eugenia Chan starts with a classic fibula pin design and adds her own twist to it by changing the shape of the pin catch and adding coil-wrapped wire in unexpected places.

FINISHED SIZE: 3" (7.6 cm)

MATERIALS

1 silver embellished copper 15x30mm bead

1 copper 14mm round bead

2 Bali silver 14mm bead caps

1 turquoise 8mm disc

2 copper 5mm rondelles

20" (50.8 cm) of round dead-soft copper 16-gauge wire

30" (76.2 cm) of round dead-soft copper 22-gauge wire

TOOLS

Flush cutters

Indelible pen

Measuring tape

0000 steel wool

Small bench block

Jeweler's flat file

Hard-plastic or rawhide mallet

Chasing hammer with convex face

Small round-nose pliers

Large round-nose pliers

Flat-nose pliers

Chain-nose pliers

STEP 1: Clean the wire with 0000 steel wool (see Basics section pp. 8–19). Wrap the 22-gauge around a 16-gauge mandrel. Cut the coil in half.

STEP 2: Flush cut (see Basics section pp. 8–19) each end to remove any sharp points. Set the coils aside.

STEP 3: Use an indelible pen to mark the 16-gauge wire 8" (20.3 cm) from one end.

STEP 4: Bend the wire at this mark, using the extra-long round-nose pliers, until it is parallel with the remaining 12" (30.5 cm) of wire.

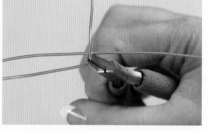

STEP 5: At 3" (7.6 cm) from the bend, bend the short wire again until it is at a 90-degree angle.

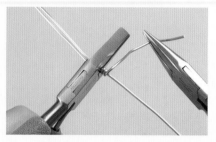

STEP 6: Hold the wire firmly in the back of the flat-nose pliers and wrap three times with the chain-nose pliers. Leave the tail end hanging.

STEP 7: Hammer the tail with a chasing hammer.

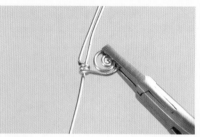

STEP 8: Spiral the wire, starting with round-nose pliers and ending with flat-nose pliers.

STEP 9: Forge the spiral with a chasing hammer on the small bench block.

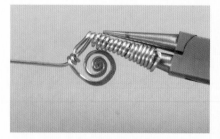

STEP 10: Pick up the fibula and place the tip of the bent wire in the middle of the large round-nose pliers. Use the pliers to bend the wire into a cone shape as shown; this forms a coiled wire catch for the point of the pin.

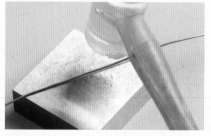

STEP 11: Hammer the remaining straight portion of the wire thoroughly with a hard-plastic or rawhide mallet to work-harden the wire (see Basics section pp. 8–19). This is especially important when working with copper wire, which is very soft.

STEP 12: Bend the wire back over the spiraled wire as shown.

STEP 13: Place 1 of the coils on the wire.

STEP 14: Use your fingers to shape the coiled wire into a U shape.

STEP 15: String the silver embellished copper bead, 1 bead cap, the copper round, 1 bead cap, 1 copper rondelle, the turquoise disc, and 1 copper rondelle on the 16-gauge wire and slide snug up against the coiled wire.

STEP 16: Place the second coil from Steps 2–3 on the 16-gauge wire and press it firmly against the beads. Bend the wire into a coiled-wire spring on the back of the extra-long round-nose pliers.

STEP 17: Place the wire tip inside the spring catch made previously. If any wire protrudes, trim it. Remove the pinpoint from the spiral catch and hammer the last ½" (1.3 cm) with a chasing hammer.

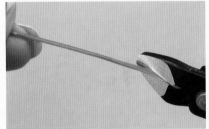

STEP 18: Use heavy flush cutters to cut the wire at an angle, forming a sharp point.

STEP 19: File the wire thoroughly, removing any rough edges.

STEP 20: Finish with a firm polish using 0000 steel wool.

COOL IDEAS!

✳ This pin looks best when artificially aged with liver of sulfur (see Basics section pp. 8–19).

✳ Coiled wire of various colors (sterling silver, brass, or craft wire) is a creative alternative to using all-copper wire.

✳ Make lots of these pins using different beads, such as handmade glass, gemstone, or metal. Look for beads with holes large enough to accommodate 16-gauge wire.

✳ Another option is to suspend handmade wire charms from the base of the pin.

COOL COPPER BANGLE

SHARILYN MILLER

Copper tubing is a great hardware-store find that makes an inexpensive and heavy-duty metal base for a chunky bangle. This design should appeal equally to men and women.

FINISHED SIZE: 9" *(24 cm)*

MATERIALS

12" (30.5 cm) of copper ¼" diameter tubing

2' (61 cm) of round dead-soft sterling silver 12-gauge wire

TOOLS

Indelible pen

Large flat file

Measuring tape

0000 steel wool

Texturing hammers

Copper tubing cutter

Small steel bench block

Small embossing hammer

Hard-plastic or rawhide mallet

Chasing hammer with convex face

Vise to attach a bracelet mandrel to a worktable

Small round-nose pliers

Large round-nose pliers

Flat-nose pliers

Chain-nose pliers

Flush cutters suitable for cutting up to 12-gauge wire

Case-hardened stainless steel bracelet mandrel, stepped

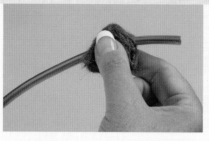

STEP 1: Measure your wrist to determine the approximate size bangle you wish to make, adding up to 2" (5.1 cm) extra to make it easier to fit the finished bangle over your hand. Run the measuring tape around the stepped bracelet mandrel to find which of the four sizes is closest to your first measurement. Write this down.

STEP 2: Gently straighten the copper tubing with your hands and clean it with 0000 steel wool (see Basics section pp. 8–19).

STEP 3: Use the measurement from the first step to mark a place on the copper tubing with an indelible pen. For example, the bangle pictured was made on the largest size and required 8" (20.3 cm) of copper tubing.

STEP 4: Use a tubing cutter to cut the copper tubing, first scoring the metal with the cutter before tightening it down to cut all the way through.

STEP 5: Use a large flat file if necessary to file away any rough edges from the cutoff piece. Set it aside.

STEP 6: Flush cut (see Basics section pp. 8–19) 2' (61 cm) of 12-gauge round dead-soft wire and clean it with 0000 steel wool. Run this wire through the copper tubing, bringing the tubing to the center of the wire. Gently bend the tubing with your thumbs to start a curve in the center. Place the end of the bracelet mandrel in a good-quality vise attached to a worktable and tighten it down securely. Place the tubing over the bracelet mandrel at your desired placement.

STEP 7: Hammer the tubing with a rawhide or hard-plastic mallet. Begin hammering from the center outward, the objective being to curve the copper tubing around the mandrel without causing a kink in the metal. Take some time with this.

STEP 8: Ensure that the wire inside the tubing is still centered with an equal amount protruding from each end. Cross the wires in the center while the tubing is still on the mandrel.

STEP 9: Place your thumbs securely on the wires, and, pressing down, twist them together. Continue twisting until a spiral emerges, finishing when the spiral is four turns around.

STEP 10: Hammer the wire spiral sharply now and again, using a hard-plastic or rawhide mallet, to keep the spiral flat.

STEP 11: Switch to a chasing hammer.

STEP 12: Now switch to texturing and embossing hammers and distress the copper tubing's surface with random marks. Repeat this exercise using the ball-peen end of your chasing hammer and other tools to artificially age the metal.

STEP 13: Remove the bracelet from the mandrel and wrap the wire ends tightly around the copper tubing, 2 to 3 wraps on each side. Press the wire down with flat-nose pliers if necessary and use chain-nose pliers to grasp the wire ends as you wrap them for a tighter fit.

STEP 14: Reserve about 2" (5.1 cm) of straight wire on each end, which will be made into decorative spirals. Forge the wire ends with a chasing or planishing hammer.

STEP 15: Grasp a wire end in the tips of the small round-nose pliers and bend the wire into a tiny loop, the beginning of a spiral. Switch to flat-nose pliers and continue spiraling in a loose, open style. Repeat with the second wire end.

STEP 16: Bend the spiral up and away from the bangle.

STEP 17: Place a spiral on the small bench block and forge it on one side, using a chasing hammer. Then use texturing and embossing hammers to create distress marks in the flattened wire. Repeat with the second spiral.

STEP 18: Use flat-nose pliers to press the spirals firmly against the copper tubing bracelet.

OPTION: Artificially aging this bracelet in hot liver of sulfur is highly recommended, as the darkening effect brings out all the distress marks in the metal (see Basics section pp. 8–19). Polish afterward with 0000 steel wool and a jewelry polishing cloth.

COOL IDEAS!

* Copper tubing and tubing cutters are readily available in most hardware stores. Be sure to purchase the ¼" (6 mm) diameter tubing, which is the ideal size for making jewelry.

* Do not substitute a wooden or plastic bracelet mandrel for case-hardened stainless steel, as these types of mandrels are too fragile for enthusiastic hammering with the chasing and texturing hammers.

* Placing heavy-gauge wire inside the tubing before you hammer it on the mandrel should greatly assist you in shaping the tubing into a rounded form without kinking the metal.

STacKED WASHER EaRRinGS

SHARILYN MILLER

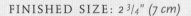

Inexpensive nuts and washers from the hardware store make intriguing components in this pair of mixed-metals earrings.

FINISHED SIZE: 2 3/4" (7 cm)

MATERIALS

2 copper color 3/8" (1 cm) coin pearls

2 steel 6mm nuts

2 yellow brass 18mm brass washers

2 copper 24mm copper washers

2 sterling silver 2" (5.1 cm) head pins

6" (15.2 cm) of round dead-soft 20-gauge wire, your choice of metal

12" (30.5 cm) of round dead-soft 18-gauge wire, your choice of metal

TOOLS

Flush cutters

Measuring tape

0000 steel wool

Small jeweler's bench block

Chasing or planishing hammer

Small ball-peen or embossing hammer

Small round-nose pliers

Large round-nose pliers

Flat-nose pliers

Chain-nose pliers

STEP 1: Use the ball-peen end of a chasing hammer or a small embossing hammer to texture one side of each copper and brass washer on a bench block. Set them aside. String a pearl onto each head pin and wrap an eye-pin loop (see Basics section pp. 8–19) at the top of each, but before closing and wrapping the loop, open it sideways and run a copper washer through it. Wrapping the eye-pin loop closed will secure it to the copper washer. Set these aside.

STEP 2: Clean all the wire thoroughly with 0000 steel wool (See Basics section pp. 8–19). Flush cut (Basics section) 8 pieces of 18-gauge wire, each 1½" (3.8 cm) long. Form the wire pieces into figure-eight links.

STEP 3: Attach 2 figure eights to each copper washer, one on each side of the pearl dangle from the previous step.

  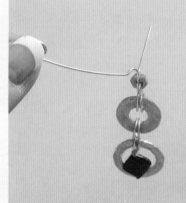

STEP 4: Attach the opposite end of the same two figure eights to yellow brass washers.

STEP 5: Attach another pair of figure eights to the yellow brass washers. Then attach the other end of each figure eight to small steel nuts. Set the pair of dangles aside.

STEP 6: Flush cut 2 pieces of 20-gauge sterling silver wire, each 3" (7.6 cm) long. Create a loop in one of the wire pieces, break the neck, and then open it sideways to insert a steel nut into the loop.

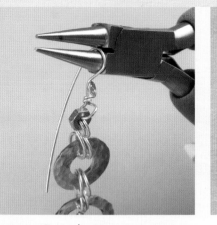

STEP **7:** Form the wire pieces into wrapped French ear wires. Wrapping the eye-pin loop closed will secure it to the nut.

COOL IDEAS!

✳ Any shape of pearl or bead will work for a bead dangle in these earrings. I like the diamond shape of these coin pearls, but circular or spherical beads or pearls would look beautiful, too.

✳ Using liver of sulfur to artificially age the finished earrings (see Basics section pp. 8–19) is a nice finishing touch. Polish the earrings carefully afterward with 0000 steel wool and jewelry polishing cloths.

SOMBRERO RiNG

SHARILYN MILLER

This is a BIG ring, no doubt about it. Maybe it's not right for every day, but it could be just the thing to wear to your next gallery opening or mariachi party.

FINISHED SIZE: *2¹/₂" (6.4 cm) diameter*

MATERIALS

6 silver head pins with decorative heads
10 Thai silver 4mm cubes
5 garnet beads
1 green garnet rondelle
3' (91.4 cm) of round dead-soft copper 18-gauge wire
4' (122 cm) of round dead-soft copper 20-gauge wire

TOOLS

Flush cutters
Measuring tape
0000 steel wool
Ring mandrel and holder
Small round-nose pliers
Large round-nose pliers
Flat-nose pliers
Chain-nose pliers

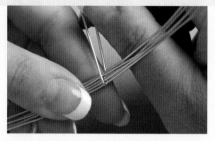

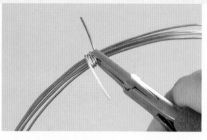

STEP 1: Clean all the wire thoroughly with 0000 steel wool. Flush cut 4 pieces of 18-gauge round wire, each piece about 8" (20.3 cm) long. Flush cut an additional piece of 18-gauge wire about 4"(10.1 cm) long. Wrap this piece of wire around the center of the 8" (20.3 cm) long wire pieces.

STEP 2: Hold the wires together side by side with flat-nose pliers as you wrap.

STEP 3: Wrap several times and then spiral in the ends for a decorative effect.

STEP 4: Wrap the 18-gauge wire pieces around the ring mandrel (your placement).

STEP 5: Twist-and-lock them together on the top.

STEP 6: To create spokes, spread out the wires in the shape of a wheel.

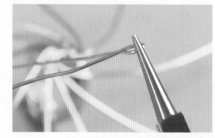

STEP 7: Flush cut 1 piece of 20-gauge wire about 4' long. Use the 20-gauge wire to twine the spokes; start by folding it in half.

STEP 8: Place the loop on any one of the spokes.

STEP 9: Wrap the wire around the next spoke in the wheel, twist, and wrap the next spoke.

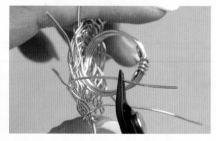

STEP 10: Continue twining around in this way until the sombrero has reached the desired size.

STEP 11: Bring each wire to the underside of the ring.

STEP 12: Flush cut the wires.

STEP 13: Spiral the ends and tuck them against the underside of the ring. Press them firmly in place with flat-nose pliers.

STEP 14: Trim the spokes so they all protrude about 3/8" (1.9 cm) from the edge of the weaving.

STEP 15: String 5 garnet beads on a head pin. String the green garnet rondelle on a head pin. Holding them together, with the rondelle in the middle, twist the wires to create a sort of "flower" of beads.

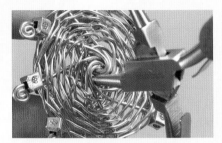  

STEP 16: If necessary, create an opening in the center of the ring using small round-nose pliers.

STEP 17: Run the wire "stems" of the flower into the center of the Sombrero ring.

STEP 18: Pull all the wires through until the flower is snug against the ring.

STEP 19: Once you've pulled all the wires through, separate them.

STEP 20: Twist and wrap each wire separately around the ring shank to hold them in place.

STEP 21: Spiral the ends and tuck them into crevices where they cannot be seen or felt.

COOL IDEAS!

✳ The appearance of this ring is easy to alter by using different beads or pearls or by using different colors of wire. Craft wire, sterling silver, and gold-filled wire are all good choices. For twining purposes, choose a soft wire that is easy to bend.

✳ A hot solution of liver of sulfur is a great way to artificially age this jewelry piece (see Basics section pp. 8–19) and give it depth and character, but it takes some time to polish afterward with 0000 steel wool.

single-loop chain

SHARILYN MILLER

Simple elegance defines this bracelet link, which is easily adaptable to necklaces as well.

FINISHED SIZE: 8" (20.3 cm)

MATERIALS

5' (152 cm) of round dead-soft copper 16-gauge wire

TOOLS

Flush cutters

Measuring tape

0000 steel wool

Small jeweler's bench block

Chasing or planishing hammer

Small round-nose pliers

Large round-nose pliers

Flat-nose pliers

Bail-forming pliers

STEP 3: Stop when the link measures 1¹/₂" (3.8 cm) from end to end.

STEP 1: Clean all of the wire thoroughly with 0000 steel wool (see Basics section pp. 8–19). Flush cut (Basics section) 4" (10.1 cm) of 16-gauge wire. Start a spiral at each end in the middle of the small round-nose pliers.

STEP 2: Use flat-nose pliers to continue the spiral on each end, facing each other.

Place the middle of the wire in the bail-forming pliers.

STEP 4: Bend the wire to create a U shape, spirals facing away from each other.

STEP 5: Use a hard-plastic or rawhide mallet to straighten and work-harden (see Basics section pp. 8–19) the wire link.

STEP 6: Use a chasing hammer to flatten the rounded wire end (the end farthest away from the spirals). Repeat these steps to make as many links as required for your bracelet. The bracelet shown has 10 links. Set them aside.

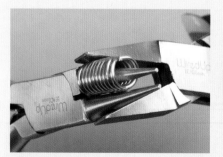

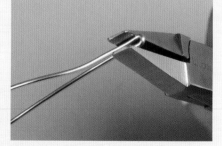

STEP 7: Create 8 or more 16-gauge small jump rings (about 5mm in diameter) plus an equal number of larger jump rings (about 8mm in diameter.), using large and small round-nose pliers. Set them aside.

STEP 8: Connect the bracelet links together using large and small jump rings as shown. Use large jump rings to connect spirals together and use doubled small jump rings to connect single-loop links back to back. Add or subtract links until the bracelet fits comfortably.

STEP 9: Create a simple hook clasp using 4" (10.1 cm) of 16-gauge wire. Begin by flush cutting 4" (10.1 cm) of 16-gauge wire and bending it in half.

STEP 10: Bend the bent wire end in the round-nose pliers to form the tip of a hook.

STEP 11: Use round-nose pliers to create a shepherd's-hook shape.

STEP 12: Form loops on the straight wire ends as shown.

STEP 13: Open the loops sideways.

STEP 14: Attach them to one end of the bracelet.

STEP 15: Close the loops and try the bracelet on, adding or subtracting links and jump rings as needed until the bracelet fits.

OPTION: Using a hot solution of liver of sulfur is recommended to give this bracelet an antique finish (see Basics section pp. 8–19).

COOL IDEAS!

✳ This link can be made in different sizes for a variety of distinctive looks. For example, try making it in 14-gauge wire (same measurements) or even 12-gauge wire (you may need to use longer lengths of wire). Or try making the same link with 4$\frac{1}{4}$" (11.4 cm) or even 4$\frac{3}{4}$" (12 cm) of wire for a very big, bold bracelet.

✳ The bracelet also can be made in sterling silver, gold-filled, or yellow brass wire.

✳ Try making several of these links and combining them with various bead wraps and other links to make a long necklace.

LEaf LINK BraCeLET

SHARILYN MILLER

Autumn leaves dance around your wrist in this pretty wire-link bracelet.

FINISHED SIZE: $7\,^3/_4$" (19.7 cm)

MATERIALS

$4\,^1/_2$' (137 cm) of round dead-soft copper 14-gauge wire

TOOLS

Flush cutters
0000 steel wool
Small steel bench block
Small embossing hammer
Chasing or planishing hammer
Hard-plastic or rawhide mallet
Small round-nose pliers
Flat-nose pliers
Chain-nose pliers

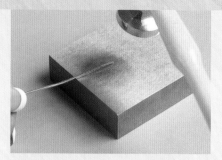

STEP 1: Clean all the wire thoroughly with 0000 steel wool (see Basics section pp. 8–19). Flush cut (Basics section) seven 6" (15 cm) pieces of 14-gauge copper wire. Flush cut one 7" (18 cm) long piece and set it aside. Pick up 1 of the 6" (15 cm) long pieces and hammer one end to flatten it using a chasing or planishing hammer.

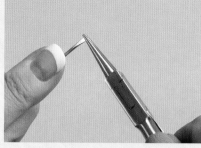

STEP 2: Place the flattened wire end in the tips of the small round-nose pliers and bend it into a small spiral.

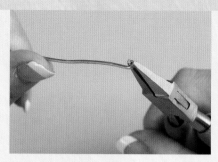

STEP 3: Switch to flat-nose pliers and tighten the beginning spiral.

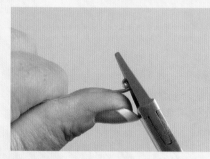

STEP 4: Continue spiraling the wire.

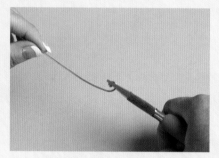

STEP 5: Spiral the wire loosely to open it up.

STEP 6: Stop when the unit is 2½" (6 cm) long from the outside of the spiral to the end of the wire.

STEP 7: Grasp the wire in the angle shown in the flat-nose pliers and bend the wire sharply against the edge of the pliers.

STEP 8: Continue spiraling around.

STEP 9: Using flat-nose pliers, bend the wire straight up from the center of the spiral, directly across the spiral from the sharp bend made in Step 7. Trim the straight wire if necessary so that it measures about ½" (1.3 cm).

STEP 10: Placing the spiraled portion of the wire only on a small jeweler's bench block, forge the outside edges of the leaf shape with a chasing or planishing hammer.

STEP 11: Switch to the small embossing hammer and forge texture into the flattened areas of the wire. If the leaf becomes misshapen, hammer it back into shape with a hard-plastic or rawhide mallet.

STEP 12: Using small round-nose pliers, form a loop in the short wire end.

STEP 13: Use chain-nose pliers to bend the loop back. Reinsert the small round-nose pliers and bend the loop slightly forward, centering it on the spiral. Repeat all of these steps with the remaining six 6" (15 cm) wire pieces. Set them aside.

STEP 14: Take the one 7" (17 cm) wire piece and hammer one end with a chasing hammer to slightly flatten it. Begin a spiral in the tips of the small round-nose pliers and then switch to flat-nose pliers. Spiral loosely until the wire measures about 3¼" (8.3 cm) long from the outside of the spiral to the end of the wire.

STEP 15: Grasp the wire in the angle shown in the flat-nose pliers and bend the wire sharply against the edge of the pliers.

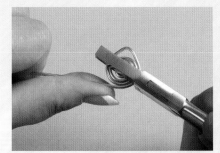

STEP 16: Continue spiraling around.

STEP 17: Using flat-nose pliers, bend the wire straight up from the center of the spiral.

STEP 18: Bend this straight wire back down toward the spiral at the midway point. Hammer and texture the leaf portion of the link as described in the previous steps.

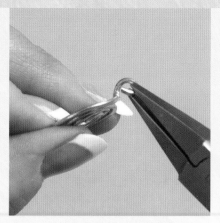

STEP 19: Place the rounded bend of wire in the back of the small round-nose pliers and bend it forward slightly.

STEP 20: Turn the wire piece around so the bent end is facing you. Place this wire end in the back of the small round-nose pliers and bend the wire up and over to form a hook.

STEP 21: To connect the leaf links, open the loops sideways.

STEP 22: Insert the loop of 1 link into the triangular shape at the bottom of another link. Repeat this step to connect all the links.

OPTION: Use a hot solution of liver of sulfur to darken your bracelet, which brings out the surface texture (see Basics section pp. 8–19). Polish with 0000 steel wool followed by a jeweler's polishing cloth.

COOL IDEAS!

✳ This bracelet looks great in different wire types such as sterling silver and yellow brass or even gold-filled. But don't try this with colored craft wire because the forging techniques used will cause the colorant to split off. Also, colored craft wire cannot be artificially aged in liver of sulfur.

✳ If you have very strong hands, try making this bracelet with 16-gauge dark annealed steel wire.

✳ Another way to change the look of this bracelet is to use longer lengths of wire or heavier gauges, such as 12-gauge or even 10-gauge, to make bigger leaves. The heavier the wire, the more you can flatten it out through forging methods. This gives you more surface area to texture with ball-peen and texturing hammers.

STICKS AND STONES EARRINGS

SHARILYN MILLER

Textured "sticks" fashioned from short wire pieces make terrific earring drops whether you use copper, yellow brass, or sterling silver to create them. Add your favorite bead or pearl dangles, and you've added an unusual fashion accessory to your wardrobe.

FINISHED SIZE: 2 7/8" (7.3 cm)

MATERIALS

2 copper 2" (5 cm) head pins
2 powder blue 6mm Czech glass beads
2 5mm peridot chips
4" (10 cm) of brass 16-gauge wire
6" (15 cm) of round dead-soft sterling silver 20-gauge wire
4" (10 cm) of copper 22-gauge wire

TOOLS

Flush cutters
Measuring tape
0000 steel wool
Small jeweler's bench block
Chasing or planishing hammer
Small ball-peen or embossing hammer
Small round-nose pliers
Large round-nose pliers
Flat-nose pliers
Chain-nose pliers

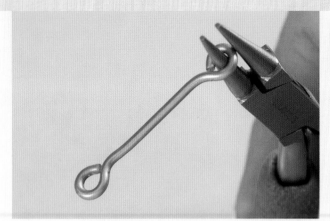

STEP 1: Clean all of the wire thoroughly with 0000 steel wool (see Basics section pp. 8–19). Flush cut (Basics section) 2 pieces of 16-gauge wire, each piece 2" (5 cm) long. Use small round-nose pliers to create a small eye-pin loop at each end of both wire pieces.

STEP 2: Place the wire across a corner of a small jeweler's bench block as shown and forge the straight portion of the wire with a chasing or planishing hammer. Repeat with the second wire piece. Switch to an embossing hammer and add texture to the forged area of each wire piece. If the wire curls up during this process, turn it over and hammer it lightly with a chasing hammer to flatten it again. Continue texturing one side of each "stick" until satisfied with its appearance. Set the textured sticks aside.

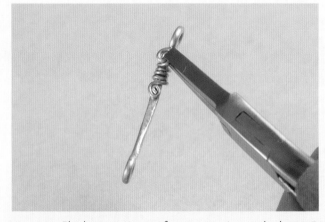

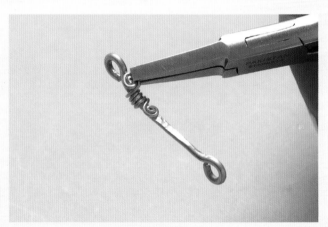

STEP 3: Flush cut 2 pieces of 22-gauge wire, each about 2" (5 cm) long. Wrap each piece around a textured stick near one of the eye-pin loops.

STEP 4: Spiral in the ends and press them tightly against the textured stick to hold them securely in place.

 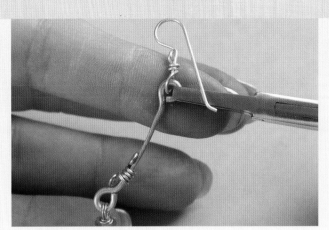

STEP 5: Use a head pin to string 1 glass bead and 1 peridot chip to create a dangle. Repeat for a second dangle. Attach each bead dangle to a textured stick by opening its eye-pin loop sideways. Close each eye-pin loop securely.

STEP 6: Flush cut the 20-gauge wire into two 3" (8 cm) pieces. Create wrapped French ear wires (see Basics section pp. 8–19) with them. Attach the ear wires to the textured sticks by opening the remaining eye-pin loops sideways. Close them securely.

OPTION: Use a hot solution of liver of sulfur to darken your Sticks and Stones earrings (see Basics section). Polish with 0000 steel wool followed by a jeweler's polishing cloth.

COOL IDEAS!

✳ Choose small beads, pearls, and/or metal beads for this project; large, heavy beads on earrings will drag on your earlobes.

✳ If the wrapped wire from Step 5 slips around and won't stay in place, a tiny drop of invisible jeweler's adhesive may be applied to the back side of the wrapped wire. Allow it to dry overnight.

✳ Textured sticks can be made any length. Try making them with 2" (5 cm) of 16-gauge wire as described above and then make several more pairs in different lengths. Try making them with different metals—sterling silver, copper, brass—and choose beads or pearls that complement the color of the metal.

✳ Textured sticks can also be made with heavier gauges of wire such as 14-gauge or even 12-gauge. As long as the wire pieces are not very long, the added weight from the heavier gauges should not be a problem. The advantage to using heavier wire is that it can be flattened out quite a bit more and textured to make a wider piece, and it makes a bolder statement.

✳ Be sure to make the eye-pin loops on each end of a wire stick prior to forging and texturing the middle of the wire. Why? Hammering metal work-hardens it (see Basics section pp. 8–19) and makes it nearly impossible to bend without breaking. If you forge and texture your sticks and create eye-pin loops on each end afterward, you will find it extremely difficult if not impossible to bend the wire.

SPiDeR-WEaVE PenDanT

SHARILYN MILLER

This Halloween-inspired woven wrap embellishes a pendant that's fun to wear any time of year. You can wear it three ways: front side (showing the weave), back side (showing the spiraled wire ends), or plain (simply remove the woven wire piece entirely).

FINISHED SIZE: *21" (53 cm)*

MATERIALS

1 30x40mm faceted stone oval

21" (53 cm) ball chain

3' (91 cm) of round dead-soft copper 22-gauge wire

7" (18 cm) of round dead-soft copper 18-gauge wire

4' (122 cm) of round dead-soft copper 24-gauge wire

TOOLS

Flush cutters

Measuring tape

0000 steel wool

Chasing hammer

Small bench block

Small round-nose pliers

Large round-nose pliers

Flat-nose pliers

Chain-nose pliers

STEP 1: Thoroughly clean your wire with 0000 steel wool (see Basics section pp. 8–19). Hammer one end of the 7" (18 cm) 18-gauge wire piece to be used for a pendant.

STEP 2: Begin a spiral at one end of the wire.

STEP 3: Press the beginning spiral tightly with the flat-nose pliers.

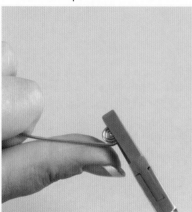

STEP 4: Continue spiraling the wire in the flat-nose pliers.

STEP 5: Once you've spiraled around three times, bend the wire straight up in a lollipop shape.

STEP 6: Hammer the spiral with a chasing hammer to flatten it slightly.

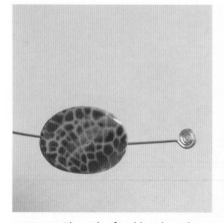

STEP 7: Place the focal bead on the wire.

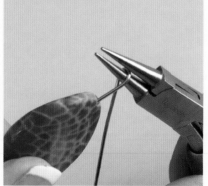

STEP 8: Begin creating a wrapped eye-pin loop (see Basics section pp. 8–19) in the wire, just above the focal bead.

STEP 9: Wrap the wire twice around the round-nose pliers.

STEP 10: Break the neck with chain-nose pliers.

STEP 11: Begin wrapping the neck, using the chain-nose pliers to wrap the wire tightly.

STEP 12: Continue wrapping the neck.

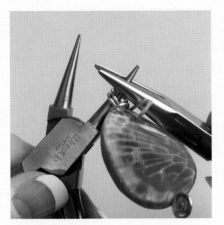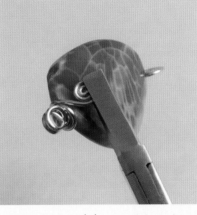

STEP 13: Equalize the loops by placing the double-wrapped eye-pin loops back on the round-nose pliers—smallest loop first. Press chain-nose pliers against the loops to force them to equalize.

STEP 14: Spiral the remaining wire end and tuck it against the focal bead with flat-nose pliers.

STEP 15: This is the finished pendant, which can be worn on a necklace chain as is, without the spider-weave wire embellishment. Set it aside for now.

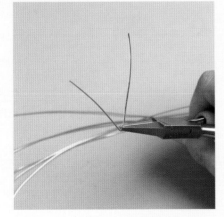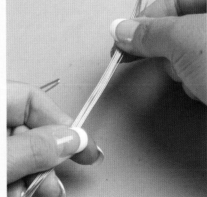

STEP 16: Flush cut (see Basics section) 6 pieces of 22-gauge wire, each 5" (13 cm) long. Reserve the remaining 4" (10 cm) of wire for wrapping; bend it in half.

STEP 17: Lay six 5" (13 cm) pieces of 22-gauge wire next to each other in a bundle.

STEP 18: Begin wrapping them in the center with the reserved 4" (10 cm) piece of wire.

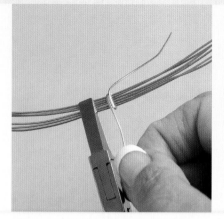 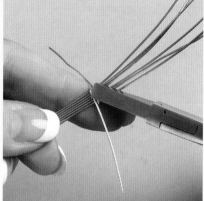 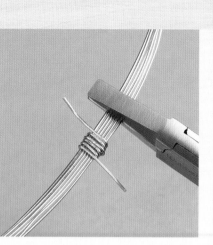

STEP 19: As you wrap the bundle, keep everything straight and flat using flat-nose pliers.

STEP 20: Use flat-nose pliers every now and then to press the wire wrap firmly against the bundle.

STEP 21: Wrap the bundle about four or five times.

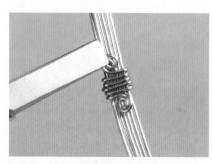  

STEP 22: Spiral in the wire ends.

STEP 23: Spread out the wire "spokes."

STEP 24: Create a tiny loop at one end of the 24-gauge wire.

 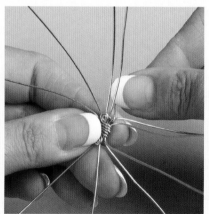 

STEP 25: Place the loop on one of the 22-gauge spokes near the center.

STEP 26: Begin wrapping the 22-gauge wire up and over each spoke, moving in a clockwise direction.

STEP 27: Wrap each spoke very tightly and make sure to keep the spokes evenly spaced as you wrap them.

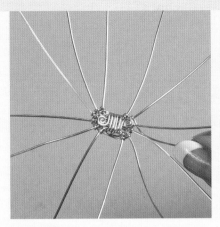

STEP 28: You will begin to see a pattern emerge. The first wrap around all the spokes is the most challenging. It becomes easier to weave after that.

STEP 29: Once you've wrapped a few times around, clip the wire with flush cutters and press the wire around a spoke to hide the cut end.

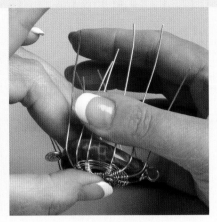

STEP 30: Place the focal bead on the weaving and bend the spokes up and around the edges of the bead.

STEP 31: Trim the spokes as needed to equalize their lengths.

STEP 32: Spiral in the ends of each spoke just a bit.

STEP 33: Press the spirals gently against the front of the focal bead. Once finished, the necklace is ready to wear. The spider-weave embellishment can be removed easily for cleaning or when you wish to wear the pendant without it.

OPTION: Use a hot solution of liver of sulfur to darken your pendant (see Basics section pp. 8–19). Polish thoroughly with 0000 steel wool followed by a jeweler's polishing cloth.

COOL IDEAS!

✳ The pendant can be made any size, but if making a very large pendant, you will need more wire.

✳ The chain you use will affect the appearance of this necklace. Possibilities include commercial chain (copper or sterling silver), a heavy-gauge neck wire, leather or satin cording, silk rattail, Buna cord, or ball chain.

✳ Sterling silver ball chain can be found in jewelry catalogs, or use steel or yellow brass ball chain from the hardware store. You may also find multicolored ball chain in the scrapbook section of your local craft store. The chain can be cut into segments of different colors and connected together with clasps as shown in the sample.

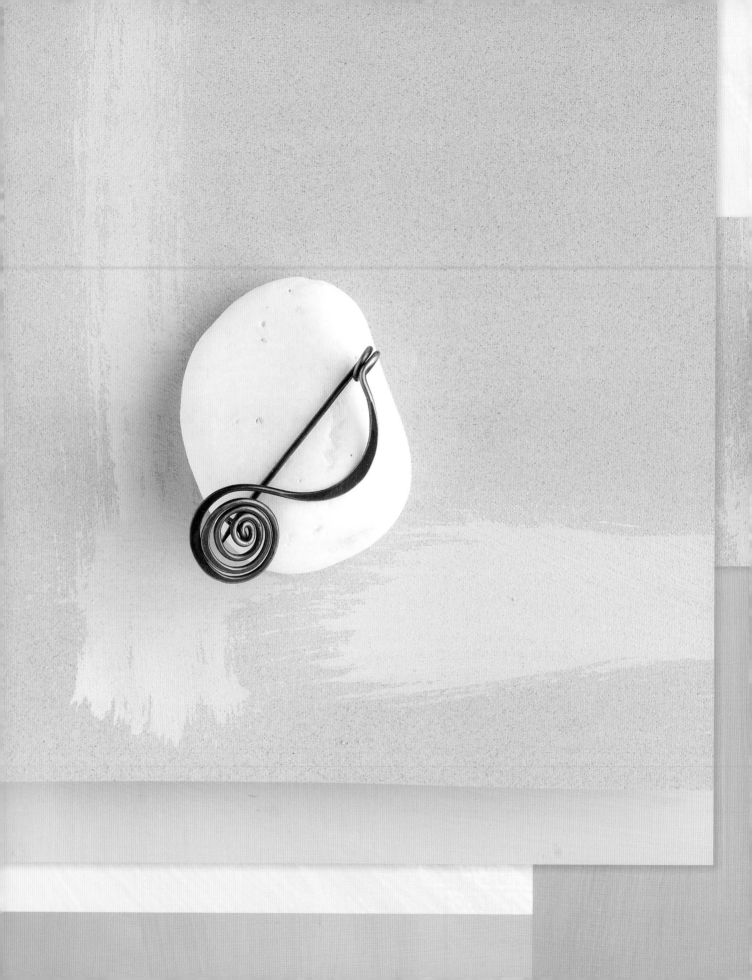

spirAL FIBULa PiN

SHARILYN MILLER

Variations on the ancient spiral fibula pin can be found in large museums around the world. It is a classic design that can be easily altered in creative ways.

FINISHED SIZE: $2^1/_4$" (5.7 cm)

MATERIALS

11" (28 cm) of round dead-soft copper 14-gauge wire

TOOLS

Measuring tape

0000 steel wool

Small bench block

Jeweler's flat file

Hard-plastic or rawhide mallet

Chasing hammer with convex face

Round-nose pliers

Flat-nose pliers

Chain-nose pliers

Flush cutters suitable for cutting up to 14-gauge wire

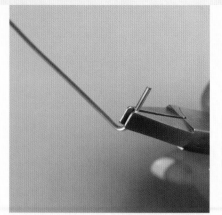

STEP 1: Flush cut (see Basics section pp. 8–19) the wire and clean it thoroughly with 0000 steel wool (Basics section). At ½" from one end, create a 90-degree bend in the wire using flat-nose pliers.

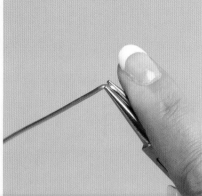

STEP 2: Place this bend in the tips of the round-nose pliers and wrap the long end of the wire around the tips of the pliers in one complete rotation.

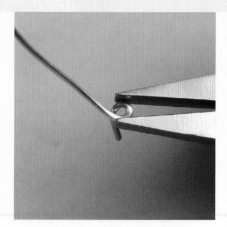

STEP 3: Remove the round-nose pliers and use flat-nose pliers to tighten the loop.

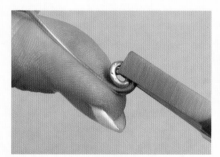

STEP 4: Place the beginning spiral in the tip of the flat-nose pliers and continue spiraling the wire tightly.

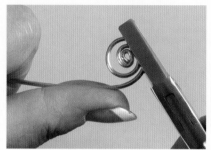

STEP 5: Loosen up the spiral.

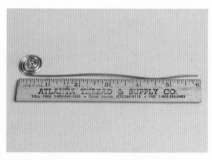

STEP 6: Continue spiraling until the unit measures 6" (15.2 cm) long from the outside of the spiral to the end of the straight wire.

STEP 7: Use your thumb to bend a smooth curve into the wire just below the spiral.

STEP 8: Forge the spiral with a chasing hammer to remove any tool marks.

STEP 9: Hammer the curve with a chasing hammer to firm up the shape and give the wire a nicely polished flat surface.

STEP 10: Use flat-nose piers to bend the wire straight up at a slight angle to the curve.

STEP 11: Bend the end of the wire protruding from the center of the spiral into a small open loop, using small round-nose pliers, to create a catch.

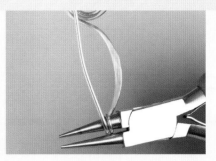

STEP 12: At the point where the wire straightens out from the curve, create a spring using the back of the small round-nose pliers.

STEP 13: To create a point on the opposite end of the wire, first flatten it slightly with a chasing hammer.

STEP 14: Cut the wire at an angle to a sharp point, using flush cutters.

STEP 15: File the wire end with a flat file.

STEP 16: Polish the tip of the pin with 0000 steel wool.

STEP 17: Make sure the tip of the pin fits into the catch perfectly.

OPTION: Artificially age the spiral fibula in liver of sulfur (see Basics section pp. 8–19).

COOL IDEAS!

* Try making this pin in copper wire first before using harder metals such as sterling silver or yellow brass.

* If you find it difficult to create the pin with 14-gauge wire, try using 16-gauge instead.

* To make a fibula with a larger spiral, use a longer length of wire and try spiraling it much looser. Be sure to reserve enough wire to create the spring and the pin.

* Beads, coil-wrapped wire, and other embellishments can be added to the pin between the spiral and the spring for a creative variation.

swinging perch earrings

SHARILYN MILLER

Small bead dangles hang gracefully from "Swinging Perch" earrings, made from small amounts of copper and sterling silver wire.

FINISHED SIZE: 2 1/8" (5.4 cm)

MATERIALS

6 round 4mm beads, gemstones, pearls, and/or metal

2 amber chips

2 turquoise 6x10mm teardrop shaped beads

2 copper 3" (8 cm) head pins

6" (15 cm) of round dead-soft 18-gauge sterling silver wire

6" (15 cm) of round dead-soft 20-gauge sterling silver wire

4 1/2" (11 cm) of round dead-soft 20-gauge copper wire

TOOLS

Flush cutters

Measuring tape

0000 steel wool

Small jeweler's bench block

Chasing or planishing hammer

Small ball-peen or embossing hammer

Small round-nose pliers

Large round-nose pliers

Flat-nose pliers

Chain-nose pliers

Large bail-forming pliers

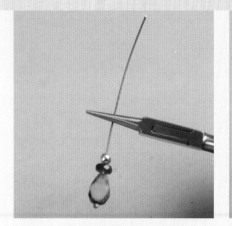

STEP 1: Start by making a bead dangle for your Swinging Perch Earrings. String 1 turquoise teardrop, 1 bead, and one 4mm round onto a 2"–3" (5–8 cm) head pin.

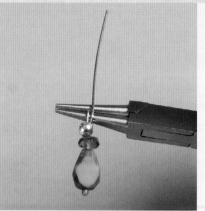

STEP 2: Wrap the wire once around small round-nose pliers.

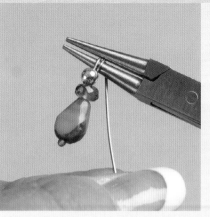

Wrap a second time around the pliers, using your fingers.

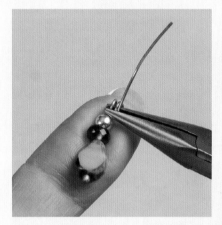

STEP 3: Break the neck, using the tips of chain-nose pliers.

STEP 4: Reinsert the round-nose pliers.

STEP 5: Place the pliers in your non-dominant hand and carefully wrap the "neck" wire above the beads, using chain-nose pliers.

STEP 6: Start a tiny spiral in the tips of the small round-nose pliers.

STEP 7: Press the spiral tightly with the tips of the flat-nose pliers.

STEP 8: Continue spiraling in the wire.

STEP 9: Tuck the spiral against the bead.

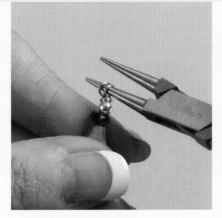

STEP 10: To equalize the loops on double-wrapped eye pins, place the loops back on the round-nose pliers, smallest loop first.

STEP 11: Grasp the tool with chain-nose pliers and press the tool firmly against the loops, forcing them to equalize. Repeat from Step 1 to make a second dangle and set them aside.

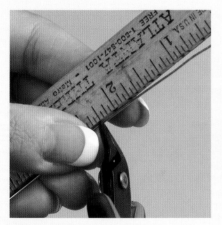

STEP 12: Flush cut (see Basics section pp. 8–19) 2 pieces of 20-gauge copper wire, each 2¼" (6 cm) long.

STEP 13: Bend a small loop on each end of both wires.

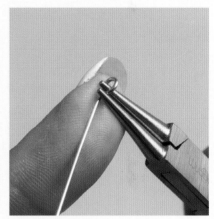

STEP 14: Break the necks to form eye-pin loops.

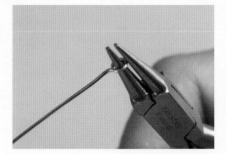

STEP 15: Center the loops on the wire ends.

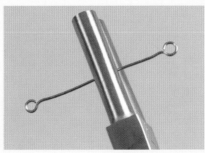

STEP 16: Use large bail-forming pliers to grasp each wire piece in the middle.

STEP 17: Bend the wire over the pliers to form a U shape.

swinging perch earrings

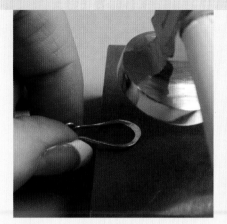

STEP **18:** Hammer the U-shaped area on a bench block, using a chasing or planishing hammer.

STEP **19:** Flush cut two 3" (8 cm) pieces of 18-gauge sterling silver wire.

STEP **20:** Start a spiral on one end of the wire, using small round-nose pliers.

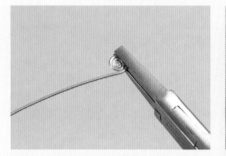

STEP **21:** Continue spiraling with flat-nose pliers.

STEP **22:** String on a small silver spacer bead, 1 of the bead dangles you made earlier, and another spacer bead. Repeat these steps with the second 20-gauge silver wire piece.

STEP **23:** Spiral in the opposite end of each wire.

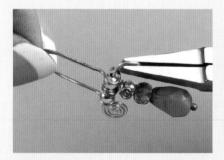

STEP **24:** Open up the eye-pin loops on the copper U-shape wire pieces and use them to attach the silver spiral component with bead dangle.

STEP **25:** Flush cut 2 pieces of 20-gauge sterling silver wire, each about 3" (8 cm) long. Form a large loop on one end of each wire piece.

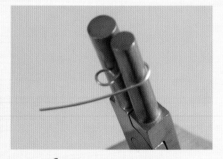

STEP **26:** Place the wire in the large bail-forming pliers and bend it over in a shepherd's hook shape. Repeat with the second wire piece.

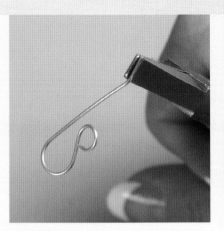

STEP 27: Bend the wire ends at a slight angle, making it easier to insert the ear wires into earlobes.

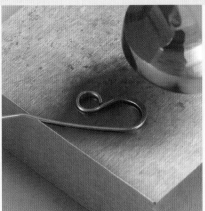

STEP 28: OPTION: Hammer the ear wires lightly with a chasing hammer.

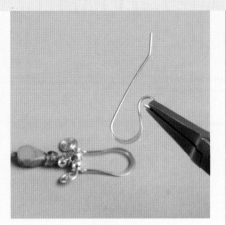

STEP 29: Open the loop on the end of the ear wire in preparation for placing a swinging perch on it.

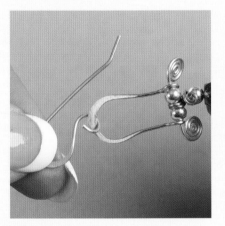

STEP 30: Place the swinging perch dangle on the ear-wire loop.

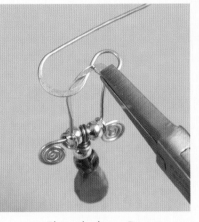

STEP 31: Close the loop. Repeat these steps with the second ear wire to make a matched pair.

OPTION: Use a hot solution of liver of sulfur to darken your Swinging Perch earrings (see Basics section pp. 8–19). Polish with 0000 steel wool followed by a jeweler's polishing cloth.

COOL IDEAS!

✳ Choose small beads, pearls, and/or metal beads for this project; large, heavy beads on earrings will drag on your earlobes.

✳ Because these earrings are made using very short wire pieces, it may be possible to make them using scrap wire leftover from larger projects.

✳ Charms, wire spirals, etc., can be substituted for bead dangles.

✳ Try making these earrings in different sizes; for example, flush cut 18-gauge wire pieces 2½" (7 cm) long instead of 2" (5 cm) long to make longer components. Also try using different metals—sterling silver, copper, yellow brass, etc.

twining vines bracelet

SHARILYN MILLER

Twisty, twining "vines" of wire lend a delicate surface embellishment to rectangular-shaped beads in this bracelet, which looks great in copper or sterling silver wire.

FINISHED SIZE: *8" (20.3 cm)*

MATERIALS

Toggle clasp

3 topaz 8mm Czech fire-polished beads

4 picture jasper 15x20mm rounded rectangles

4' (122 cm) of round dead-soft copper 18-gauge wire

18" (46 cm) of round dead-soft copper 22-gauge wire

TOOLS

Flush cutters

0000 steel wool

Small jeweler's flat file

Small steel bench block

Chasing or planishing hammer

Small round-nose pliers

Flat-nose pliers

Chain-nose pliers

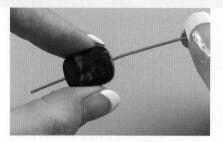 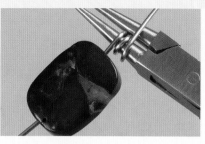 

STEP 1: Clean all the wire thoroughly with 0000 steel wool (see Basics section pp. 8–19). Test your rectangular-shaped beads to see if 18-gauge wire will pass through the bead holes. If not, substitute 20-gauge wire for the 18-gauge wire requirement.

STEP 2: Flush cut (see Basics section pp. 8–19) 4 18-gauge (or 20-gauge) wire pieces, each 10" (25.4 cm) long. About one-third down the wire, wrap the wire twice around the middle of the round-nose pliers.

STEP 3: Break the neck as shown.

STEP 4: Wrap the neck once or twice around.

STEP 5: Place a rectangular bead on the long wire end and create another double-wrapped eye-pin loop, wrapping the neck tightly. Bring both long wire ends to one side of the bead.

STEP 6: Cross the wires in the center of the bead and press them tightly against the bead surface.

  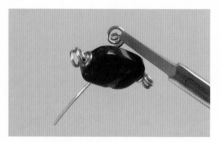

STEP 7: Twist the wires a few times, creating a spiral and simultaneously pressing the wire down firmly against the bead.

STEP 8: Hammer each wire end with a chasing hammer.

STEP 9: Spiral them both in, starting with small round-nose pliers and finishing with flat-nose pliers.

STEP 10: Forge the spirals if desired. Tuck the spirals against the bead.

STEP 11: Repeat with remaining wire and beads. Line up to see how they will look as a bracelet.

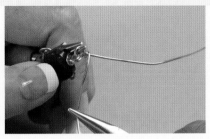

STEP 12: Flush cut three 22-gauge wire pieces, each about 6" (15.2 cm) long. About one-third down the wire, form a small eye-pin loop in the middle of the small round-nose pliers. Before closing the loop, attach 1 of the wire-wrapped rectangle beads made earlier.

STEP 13: Close the loop and wrap the neck.

Thread a fire-polished bead on the long end of the wire.

STEP 14: Create a loop in the wire near the bead but before closing it, attach a wir-wrapped rectangle bead.

STEP 15: Wrap the necks to secure the bead in place.

STEP 16: Spiral in the ends. Repeat the above steps until you have a linked bracelet that is about an inch too short to fit around your wrist.

STEP 17: Using 18-gauge wire, create 3 small jump rings to attach to each end of the bracelet.

STEP 18: Attach the toggle clasp.

OPTION: Use a hot solution of liver of sulfur to darken your bracelet (see Basics section pp. 8–19). Polish with 0000 steel wool followed by a jeweler's polishing cloth.

COOL IDEAS!

✳ To vary the look of this bracelet, try using larger beads or heavier gauge wire.

✳ Look for beads with large surface areas to embellish with spiraled wire ("twining vines"). Smaller beads are not as useful because they are easily overwhelmed with too much wirework.

✳ Add a counterweight bead near the end of the bracelet to keep it from riding up on your wrist.

SPIRaL HOOK EaRRINGS

SHARILYN MILLER

Unusual spiral-shaped hook earrings are matched with triangle-spiral charms and bead dangles.

FINISHED SIZE: 1 3/4" (4 cm)

MATERIALS

4 copper head pins with ball heads

2 labradorite 8mm rondelles

2 Thai silver 4mm cornerless cubes

2 Thai silver 4mm cubes

4 silver 4mm rounds

2 7x10mm garnets

16" (41 cm) of round dead-soft copper 20-gauge wire

8" (20.3 cm) of round dead-soft copper 18-gauge wire

TOOLS

Flush cutters

Measuring tape

0000 steel wool

Small jeweler's bench block

Chasing or planishing hammer

Small round-nose pliers

Large round-nose pliers

Flat-nose pliers

Chain-nose pliers

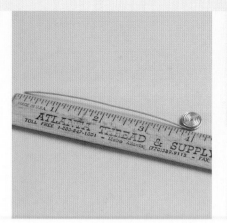

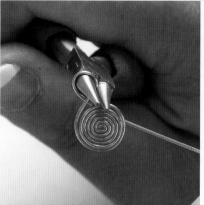

STEP 1: Clean all of the wire thoroughly with 0000 steel wool (see Basics section pp. 8–19). Flush cut (see Basics section) 2 pieces of 20-gauge wire, each 8" (20 cm) long. Spiral in one end of each wire piece until it measures 4" (10 cm) long from the outside of the spiral to the end of the wire.

STEP 2: On the back of the spiral, with small round-nose pliers, bend the wire up and over in a loop.

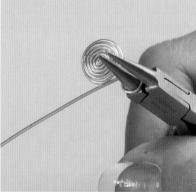

STEP 3: Change the orientation of the tool so that you can wrap the wire completely around it as shown. Repeat from Step 1 with the second wire piece.

STEP 4: Switch to chain-nose pliers and bend the wire around the outside of the spiral.

STEP 5: Bend the wire straight up from the spiral. Repeat with the second spiral.

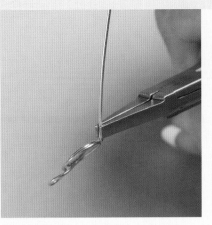

STEP 6: Bend the wire forward as shown. Repeat Steps 4–6 with the second spiral.

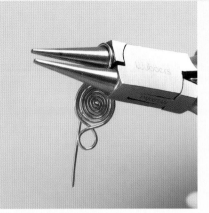

STEP 7: Bend the wire up and over the back of the large round-nose pliers to form an ear hook. Repeat with the second spiral. Bend the last ¹/₄" (2 cm) of wire up just a little to create a tail that easily inserts into your earlobe. File the wire end or use a cup burr in a handheld drill to smooth it. Repeat this step with the second wire piece, and you have two spiral-hook earrings. Set these aside.

STEP 8: Create 4 bead dangles as shown in the Basics section. Use 1 cornerless cube, 1 labradorite rondelle, and 1 silver round to create 2 of the dangles. Use 1 purple bicone and 1 silver round to create 2 of the dangles. Set them aside. Flush cut 2 wire pieces of 18-gauge wire, each 4" (10 cm) long. Use them to make 2 triangle-spiral charms as shown in the Basics section; beads are optional. To assemble the earrings, pick up a spiral-post earring from Steps 2–7 and use flat-nose pliers to open the loop on the spiral sideways.

STEP 9: Insert 1 bead dangle, 1 triangle-spiral charm, and 1 more bead dangle onto the wire. Run them around until they fit inside the eye-pin loop at the bottom of the spiral. Using flat-nose pliers, close the spiral firmly.

COOL IDEAS!

* Since several beads dangle from each earring, use small, lightweight beads or pearls that won't drag on your earlobes.

* Artificially aging your earrings in a hot solution of liver of sulfur helps to unify the design, especially if you used mixed metals such as silver and copper.

* If you can't wear copper in your earlobes, substitute sterling silver wire to make spiral-hook earrings. Another option is to give each ear wire a light coat of clear nail polish. Allow it to dry 24 hours before inserting the wire into your earlobe.

ResouRCes

Copper washers, metal hole punches, hammers, inexpensive tools:

Harbor Freight
harborfreight.com

Copper tubing, tubing cutters, metal washers and nuts (brass, steel, etc.):

Various hardware stores

Sterling silver, copper, gold, gold-filled, brass wire:

Metalliferous
metalliferous.com

Monsterslayer
monsterslayer.com

Rio Grande
riogrande.com

Thunderbird Supply
thunderbirdsupply.com

Copper, yellow brass, annealed steel wire:

Various hardware stores

Fishing tackle boxes (for organizing beads and findings):

basspro.com

Colored craft wire:

artisticwire.com
parawire.com

Jewelry tools (pliers, cutters, specialty hammers and mallets, files, bench blocks, wire gauge measuring tool, ring and bracelet mandrels, etc.):

Otto Frei
ottofrei.com

Rio Grande
riogrande.com

Thunderbird Supply
thunderbirdsupply.com

Wired Up Beads
wiredupbeads.com

Rubber lacing, ball chain, inexpensive chains, plastic bead storage boxes, small plastic bags:

Jo-Ann Fabrics & Crafts
joann.com

Michaels Arts & Crafts
michaels.com

Specialty cutters and pliers:

Tronex Tools
tronextools.com

Wired Up Beads
wiredupbeads.com

Liver of sulfur (LOS):

Rio Grande
riogrande.com

Thunderbird Supply
thunderbirdsupply.com

CONTRIBUTING ARTISTS

The following wire-jewelry and mixed-media artists contributed their designs to this book and can be reached at their respective websites:

Dale "Cougar" Armstrong
cougarscreations.com

Eugenia Chan
eugenia-c.com

Sharilyn Miller
sharilynmiller.com

Rachel Nelson-Smith
msrachel.com

Richard Salley
rsalley.com

INDeX

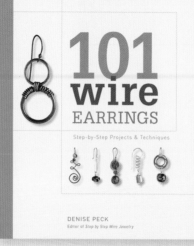
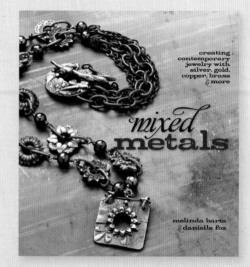